TRANSFORMATION

Reinventing Selling for Breakthrough Results

by

Best Selling Author

Bob Beck

ISBN: 1480263176
ISBN 13: 9781480263178

Table of Contents

TRANSFORMATIONAL QPQ SELLING

CHAPTER 4
Transformational QPQ SELLING CASE STUDIES **57**

CHAPTER 5
DEVELOPING MUTUAL RESPECT with QPQ **79**

CHAPTER 6
THE VALUE OF NO 99

CHAPTER 7
CREATIVITY 115

CHAPTER 8
TRANSFORMATION IN COMMUNICATION
SOCIAL MEDIA 133

CHAPTER 9
HANDLING OBJECTIONS 149

CHAPTER 10
TROUBLESOME TRUTH 159

What Our Transformed Clients Say

"The QPQ approach to selling helped us survive as a company. You gave us the tools, or we wouldn't have survived otherwise. That's a pretty good outcome, I'd say."

Mitch Copman, President, Classic Real-Estate Systems

"The new sales process had a direct impact on our ability to close over $12 million in new contracts in 2011 and is helping us accelerate new business in 2012. I expect the number of deals and total revenue in new incremental business this year to be even greater as a result of the new sales process and cadence."

Brad Cates, President, Standard Register Healthcare

"Using the QPQ approach, our average deal size is up by 44 percent over the same period last year, and new account growth is up by 90 percent over the same time period. We have achieved all these results with a 60 percent forced turnover of the sales force. I personally, along with the rest of our team, attribute much of our success this year to Ross's use of the new approaches."

Rick Marquardt, President, Ross Systems

"One of the biggest gaps today in selling is a lack of discipline to define a sales process that is mutually agreed to by the sales team and the customer. With QPQ, Bob created the guiding principles to allow our teams to follow a deal process that held everyone accountable to execution, including the customer. Not only did QPQ bring revenue results, it created a standardized methodology for everyone in the organization, streamlining the way we reviewed and managed deals."

Deb Cupp, Vice President, Healthcare Sales SAP

"I have to tell you that I was very pleasantly surprised at what I saw in your QPQ selling class. The QPQ approach is the best I have ever seen and has opened my eyes to many new, practical ways to grow our revenues."

Bob Neely, Vice President of Sales, Syntex

"Within one day of completing the course, my team uncovered two opportunities by applying the techniques they learned. The result was $300,000 of closed business inside of thirty days that previously was not even on our radar!"

Robert Lasher, President, Application Partners

"As you know the last couple of years we had other sales-training courses, but your real-life, practical, and tactical approach will net us the results we need."

Lawson Y. Glenn, Director, Global Alliances, Indus International

"As Computer Associates' top sales representative for three years in a row under the interBiz e-business applications division, I found your Quid Pro Quo Selling training as a whole new revenue opportunity for my continued success."

L. Scott Donnelly, Sales Executive, Computer Associates

"After taking many sales-training courses, I found that this was one of the few classes that actually helped reps build a pipeline and help them work through the pipeline."

Bob Lastorka, Federal Business Development Manager, Optio Software

"Using the QPQ tactics helped me close three to four deals last year, totaling around $400,000 in software, and achieving an overall 119 percent of quota. I am not sure these deals would have closed without using this strategy and making sure that all bases were covered."

Amanda P. Torbett, Senior Account Manager, CDC Software

"I really enjoyed the time we spent together. The QPQ Sales process and support on deal reviews really made the difference on so many deals we closed. Much of what you showed me has become a best practice in business development, so I thank you for that."

Bob Paradise, National Sales Manager for Enterprise Sales, Standard Register

"It wasn't until after we did the workshop that I realized the full value that Quid Pro Quo Selling brings to the table. The last thing our sales and account execs, who are all seasoned veterans, wanted was more time wasted in yet another sales-training class. By noon of the first day, they couldn't stop talking about Quid Pro Quo. While your approach is direct, practical, and based on undeniable logic, it was totally different than any training we'd seen before. There wasn't a single person who didn't buy into the QPQ approach."

Amy Phelps, Vice President, Sales Operations, SAP Public Services

"I directly attribute Systems Conversion Ltd. making the Inc. 500 list of fastest-growing privately held companies to the strategies, training, and consulting that the QPQ approach provided us."

Jeff Culverhouse, CEO, Systems Conversion Limited

"Using the QPQ approach, we now have a proven, credible process for accessing executive levels within our prospect's organization. Most importantly, we have a very clear picture of how to communicate and position our solutions in the marketplace."

Gene Hindman, President, Offset Atlanta

"I sincerely appreciate everything you have done for me over the past couple of years. With your input and guidance, I was positioned for multiple promotions with additional responsibility, making a positive impact while transforming the healthcare business."

Derek P. Carbone, Sales Director, Standard Register

Dedications

This book is dedicated to all sellers around the world who struggle every day to be the best they can be. This especially is dedicated to the "QPQ Disciples" who apply the approach and who have been transformed by their improved results. Last, but not least, this book is dedicated to my wife, Laurie and four children, who inspire me daily.

Introduction

When I was ten years old my family moved from Columbus, Ohio, to Cincinnati, Ohio. I left all my friends and all my sports teams, and I had to start in a new school where everyone was a stranger. There was no doubt in my mind my life was over. For the next several months all I heard over and over again from my parents was, "The only thing you can count on in life is change." I hated that saying, and it certainly didn't help me adjust to my new surroundings. It didn't help me because I didn't accept it or embrace the changes that were required in my life. The second I accepted and embraced the changes is when my life transformed. I made new friends, was on better sports teams, met a girl and fell in puppy love, and my life was a celebration.

Depending on your grown-up perspective, change is what you make of it. Change is happening every day regardless of where you live, what your role in life is, who you work for, or whether you want it or not. The more you ignore the opportunities that change offers you, the harder it will be for you to experience a positive transformation.

Instead of hearing about the new things sales reps are doing to improve their results the common reasons for the lack of results I hear are: that the markets are soft, the products are overpriced, and the organization is not supportive. As much as sales professionals need to change their approach, we see organizations that are not transforming to keep pace with current market conditions. It is easy to see the problem, and why production across the board is down.

Anyone who sells anything will benefit from this book. The purpose of this book is to introduce new, fresh tactics that will bring fun, pride, and consistent results back to selling. The Transformational QPQ Sales approach will give you a well-defined, systematic, and repeatable process that will raise your sales to a new level. By applying this approach using aggressive, professional, and creative sales skills (which I'll teach you), you'll enjoy sales success that far exceeds your expectations.

Throughout this book, we'll address each specific area of sales to help you maximize your opportunity. I'll provide creative solutions to each obstacle you may face. The Transformational QPQ Sales approach is designed to give you valuable tools you can utilize immediately and that will serve you throughout your sales career. Unlike so many other books, courses, and workshops, we will go into practical detail of how using the QPQ approach will give you a repeatable and predictable process. In my experience, most alternatives offer the theory of selling but are very difficult to apply. Regardless of what you sell, you will find QPQ to be universally accepted. It doesn't matter what experience level you have. We have had career sales experts come out of our workshops shocked that they learned many new things that gave them break-through results. If you are just starting out in sales, read this book, so you start off doing the right things.

Keep in mind that this is not your father's sales approach (unless you are one of my kids). With all the changes going on in business, it is a requirement that you adopt a new approach to selling to transform your results. Sellers must change their perspectives and display cour-age when pursuing new business opportunities. Merely reading this book is easy and is not enough. Becoming disciplined enough to adopt and transforming to apply-ing the principles of the QPQ approach on a daily basis may challenge you.

You've probably heard that it takes three weeks to form a habit. A habit can turn into a discipline. If you dis-cipline yourself and hold yourself accountable on a daily basis to the tactics in this book, something magical will happen. The magic will be a positive transformation in your results.

My suggestion is you outline this book, take notes, and refer to it over and over again. That way this book will affect your sales career and offer you an approach that will transform your results. If you work through a little pain, I promise you'll see a little transformation, then more transformation, then a significant and potentially life-changing transformation.

CHAPTER 1

TRANSFORMATION AND CHANGE

You might be asking yourself, "Why would a book about transforming your results and selling start with change?" The definition of transformation is a change or an alteration of something. Constant transformation and change is how the world turns. "What you're supposed to do when you don't like a thing is change it. If you can't change it, change the way you think about it." Maya Angelou

The world we live in has certainly changed over the last couple of years. Regardless of what market space you are in, it has changed too. Most people would agree that the way business is done has changed, and is transforming. This being the case, it only makes logical sense that you need to change your sales approach. If you are in an organization that adopted a sales methodology a few years ago, or an individual who is approaching prospects/sales pursuits the same way as you always have, then you might consider making some changes. On the other hand, if you are exceeding all your revenue goals and are achieving your full potential, then there's no need to change a thing. However, I haven't met a CEO or sales professional in any field who has said he/she was doing *that* well. So it's time to consider a transformation in all aspects of your sales approach. This would also be prudent for all revenue-generation activities and maybe your general outlook, if you are going to keep pace with everything that is changing around you.

You probably have already learned Albert Einstein's definition of insanity: doing the same thing over and over again and expecting a different result. No one can argue the pure and straightforward logic behind that statement. Every time I have quoted this age-old definition of insanity, everyone smiles. People tend to nod their heads, acknowledging they know that definition. What they are essentially saying without speaking is that the phrase certainly does not apply to them. However, in my experiences dealing with large groups of salespeople around the world, that quote might apply to the sales profession more than any other occupation. Salespeople as a general rule are notorious for investing their time and energy into the same activities quarter after quarter, year after year, whether it nets them the results they want or not.

For example, have you ever started a new job or gone into a new territory and spent countless hours dialing for dollars—cold calling? If you are in sales, I know the answer is yes. Let's say you spent 50 percent of your time on this activity and only got a 5 percent return on your efforts. Let's take this further and say that the 5 percent return did not net the results that met your quota expectations. As you were reviewing your results in your one-on-one session with your manager, I'd bet you had statements like, "It's early in the game," "The territory is dead," "I'm not having a lot of success getting through—just getting voicemails and being blocked by gatekeepers." Your objectives in this meeting are to convince your manager that things will turn around next quarter and that you will be back on track real soon. You do an excellent job, and your manager buys into everything you have said. She/he makes a couple of suggestions for you, and you are back in the game, hunting for new opportunities to achieve your quota.

What I see time and time again in this scenario is that the sales reps change hardly anything they are doing. They continue executing the same way they did in the previous quarter that was not achieving the required results. They keep doing the same thing over and over, hoping something will change. In this case, they kept banging the phones, with no change in their talk track, the level of the person they are calling, or sometimes even the calling list being used. Every once in a while, they stumble on a big opportunity, but as the saying goes, a blind squirrel finds a nut every once in a while too. If you want your results to change, you have to change some of the things you are doing. This simple idea applies in all aspects of our lives and is one of the principles that successful people follow. Change is constant and is never ending.

OLD MAN

My youngest son, Nick, was a terrific varsity high school tennis player. He had many lessons growing up and started playing at a young age. He went to the regional championships his senior year. I too play a lot of tennis and have played for many years. Nick and I get out a couple of times a week and play a spirited few sets of singles. For years, Nick couldn't beat me. Technically, his form and strokes are better than mine. He can hit the ball harder, and he has had hundreds more lessons than I have had. The fact that I am thirty years older than Nick plays a factor in the outcome as well. I took a lot of pleasure in rubbing my victories in his face: "Nick, I am thirty years older than you, never had a lesson, yet I still beat you like a rented donkey!" Suddenly, though, the games got closer and closer until one day he beat me! "Take that, old man!" Old man? Who was he talking to? Nick had made some changes in the way he was playing me. He figured out he better get his first serve in, because I would tee off every time on his weak second serve. He improved his serve in general, and he hit more and more balls to my backhand. He took some pace off the ball and stopped over hitting. He started beating me regularly, like every time we played! Guess who needed to change now?

Many organizations need to adopt change and look hard at what they are doing too. Many companies we work with at the Transformation-Group (www. Transformation-Group.com) fall prey to the Pot Roast Syndrome.

POT ROAST SYNDROME

The story of the pot roast goes like this: There was a young married couple who have their family over for Christmas dinner for the first time. The husband's favorite meal is pot roast. He walks into the kitchen just as his wife is cutting off the end of the pot roast. He exclaims, "Why are you cutting off the butt end of the pot roast? That's the best part." His wife is now startled and perplexed with his outburst. She replies, "I do that because my mom always did it that way." The young couple goes on the hunt to find Mom now. After they find her, the young wife asks, "Mom, why do we cut the butt end of the pot roast off before we cook it?" Mom stares into space for a second and then replies, "That is the way Grammy always did it." Of course, they go find Grammy and ask her, "Why do we cut the butt end of the pot roast off before we cook it?"

Without missing a beat, Grammy replies, "I'm not sure why you guys do it. I just never had a pan that was big enough for the entire pot roast."

I feel the Pot Roast Syndrome is one of the biggest issues organizations face. Often the senior management team fails to recognize this syndrome. Organizations keep doing things the same way because that's how they have always done them. There are so many processes and procedures that are just outdated and antiquated, yet they don't get changed. Just today my wife told me about her friend who bought a lot in a neighborhood down the street. Before anyone can build a home, he/she has to get the architectural plans approved by the homeowners association, which has a list of architects you have to use. There were many delays in getting this list to our friends, which set them back many weeks from when they wanted to start building. Once they did get the list, 70 percent of the architects were no longer in business. But that had always been the list, and they just kept handing it out year after year with no changes.

JUST BECAUSE

You might think the above situation wouldn't happen on your watch and that someone was just not paying attention. Maybe, but one more of many examples I could cite of this syndrome was uncovered on one of our organizational assessments. Depending on the challenges, goals, and scope of the project, the first thing we typically do at TG (Transformation Group) is conduct these organization assessments. Not unlike a doctor, we ask a lot of questions to determine the issues. With the answers, we develop the best course of action to improve the results. On this particular engagement, the company had been in business for several years. It was making money, but the growth was way too slow. An issue we uncovered was how it priced its product. It had a product selling for $2,350. I happened to know a little bit about the market and felt pretty sure that price was too low.

Not wanting to be too presumptuous, I sat with the CEO and asked him why his price was $2,350 for the product. He proudly replied, "We raised it from $1,750 last year." Of course, that didn't answer my question, so I asked how they knew raising the price to $2,350 was the right price for the market. Again, he confidently replied, "That is what the market will bear." We had done our research and knew that was not correct. The fact was the company had just fallen into the habit of pricing its products low, and it had never tested the market. It hadn't considered the real value it was offering its prospects and clients.

This was just another version of the Pot Roast Syndrome. This company and CEO had just always priced their product low, were selling it, and were making a little money, so they never even questioned their pricing. After many meetings with objection after objection from the management team, I convinced them to raise the price. We raised the price from $2,350 to $25,000! There were no new features added and no additional services or promises. We just raised the price. Of course, the executive team and sales team felt the market wouldn't bear an increase of that magnitude. They were afraid they would sell less volume. The fact was they could afford to sell a lot less volume. They would still be way ahead at the $25,000 price point. Amazingly, they sold more solutions at $25,000 than they did at $2,350!

Prospects perceived more value at $25,000 than at the basement price of $2,350. The story doesn't end there, though. After a couple of years, I suggested they move their price up again to $80,000! Again, a lot of meetings, convincing, and justifications took place explaining the need for higher prices. Keep in mind this is the same product with *no* enhancements or features that they were selling for $2,350. To be fair, we had changed their sales approach and messaging and transformed the sales organization to more of a solution-orientated sales team instead of an inside sales group.

Stop and think about the transformation this company went through and the success it enjoyed by transforming in this way. Its revenues increased by a factor of seven, it had a successful initial public offering, and the CEO is now sitting in South Florida learning how to fly his new plane. I bet he even has a pan big enough for any size pot roast he wants.

TRANSFORMATION AND CHANGE

It isn't easy to change something you have been doing for a long time, especially if it has brought you success in the past. The one thing you can truly count on in your life is change. Nothing ever stays the same. You have to be flexible enough to change with the situations you have. That includes selling, tennis, relationships, and every other aspect of your life.

CATALYST TO TRANSFORMING YOUR SUCCESS

You are the catalyst to transforming your level of success. To be successful and have a fulfilling career, you have to take charge and make key decisions. Only you can be the catalyst to success. No one but you can create the success you want for yourself. To start this journey, you will need to examine your past experiences and goals and determine what is working for you and what is not. If you're not accustomed to the techniques used in self-examination, you may become impatient and start the blame game. It is not unusual for sales professionals to look outwardly and blame their lack of results on everything other than themselves. I often hear things like "the market is lousy," "the product is weak," "my boss is a jerk," "the company is not supportive,". When things aren't going exactly as you would like, you have to embark on a journey of self-reflection. By doing this, you will discover the changes you need to make, which will enable you to achieve anything you want.

HOW TO ACHIEVE YOUR FULL POTENTIAL

Core Concepts of Transformational Change

- Realizing how to achieve your full potential
- Building self-awareness
- Identifying what is not working
- Knowing how to benefit from change
- Leveraging your unique skills

In this chart these concepts are essential if you're going to reach your full potential, but unfortunately, you've probably never learned about them. To understand these concepts, you will have to develop a self-awareness process. You need to examine yourself to determine what truly matters to you, without your ego getting in the way. We all have to push ourselves to new levels and be willing to try new things if there is any chance in to realize our full potential.

UNDERSTANDING SELF-AWARENESS

You should work hard to develop a discipline of self-awareness. When you do this it may become clear what is really going on. Back to the above example, let's say you aren't working closely enough or early enough in the sales cycle with decision makers. Perhaps you aren't comfortable with decision makers because you don't thoroughly understand them, you might be afraid of rejection, you have issues with authority figures, or you find them too difficult to reach. The first step is to recognize something isn't working; the next step is sorting out why. This step can be challenging and sobering. The answer almost always points back to you, which means you have to change. For most of us, change is against human nature. It is easier to stay with something we know, even if it is not working, versus venturing off into the unknown and trying something new. Now you can see the foundation for the definition of insanity. I have yet to find someone who will admit the definition applies to him/her.

IDENTIFYING WHAT'S NOT WORKING

From a sales perspective, if you can be just a little bit honest with yourself, it is pretty easy to know what's not working. If you are not getting the consistent results you want, something isn't working. There are two things you need to do to figure out what's not working. First and foremost, take an inward view. Look at the person in the mirror first. Regardless of who you are, what company you work for, and your position in the company, you will *always* find some issues that can impact your performance and results.

The question is, "Are the issues you find in one of these areas the real reason you aren't achieving the results you want?"

TRANSFORMATION

If the answer is no, then the second step is to determine what is not working that you have control over. To do this, you have to measure yourself and know what you are doing. The first thing to do is keep track of how you are spending your time. This is a detailed exercise. Below is a chart you can use that will help you sort out what's not working and why. Make a chart for every day of the week. After you list the activity, record the number of hours you spent on that activity, and then assign a number one through ten for each of the last three columns. One is the best, and ten is the worst.

TRANSFORMATION CHANGE CHART

ACTIVITY	AMOUNT OF TIME SPENT	DEGREE OF DIFFICULTY	HAPPINESS FACTOR	MOVING ME FORWARD

Degree of difficulty will tell you how hard you think something is. The tasks we find challenging are the ones we tend to shy away from doing. Ask yourself if there is anything you can do to make that task easier, like getting additional training or getting help from someone.

Happiness factor is simply measuring how happy a certain task makes you. Things that make us happy are generally fun, and we like to do them. If they don't make us happy, we don't do them as well, and we are likely to avoid them. Success does not have to involve a lot of suffering and unhappiness. It always surprises me when people debate that statement with me. I'm not saying it's a party every day. If people are generally unhappy doing something, they will avoid it. When this occurs, they need to figure out how they can feel better about whatever it is that's making them feel that way.

Moving me forward is where it all comes together. Is the activity you are investing in moving you closer or farther away from your goals? Is that activity netting you the results you want and need? You might have an activity that you rate low on the degree of difficulty and high on the happiness factor, but if it is not moving you forward, then you can't keep doing that action. Your other choice is to determine how to get better at that activity so it does move you forward. You have to create a specific and detailed improvement plan.

You might love networking, and meeting new people makes you happy. You might be spending ten hours a week, or 25 percent of your time, networking, but thus far you have not gotten one new opportunity from doing this. Either you have to replace this activity, take back 25 percent of your time, and start doing something that will bring you results, or figure out why your networking skills are not bringing you any business.

I will absolutely promise that if you are diligent and commit to filling out the Change Chart for just one week, it will become clear what you need to change. If you can stick with it for a month, the required changes you need to make will hit you in the face like a ninety-mile-an-hour fastball. It will be painful at first, but you won't let that ball keep hitting you in the face!

HOW TO BENEFIT FROM CHANGE

It has been said that the only things we can count on are death and taxes. I'll add a third thing to that list: change. This is a constant in our lives. On a basic level, we change jobs, careers, partners, cities, and more. On a more intellectual level, it is my perception that changes take place on a daily basis. Pat Croce, owner of the Philadelphia 76ers, summed it up when he said, "No one ever stays the same. You're either getting better or you're getting worse. But simply knowing and accepting this gives you the opportunity to make your changes positive ones."

Positive change starts with positive thinking. Positive thinking is a choice. To move forward, negativity must be banished. When you stop and think about it, how do most people view change, any change? How would you feel if you read a company memo right now that stated your quota was increasing by 25 percent, or you were getting a new territory, or the organization was adopting a new sales approach and process? Most people resist change at all cost. They get stuck doing things the same way and create a comfort zone with a big wall around it. There's no benefit in doing that. Change is happening in your life and your organization right now. You can view change as a defeating inconvenience or as an opportunity to grow and thrive. How you benefit from change will depend on your attitude and actions.

Positive thinking can change the outcome of any situation in your life. Everyone knows someone with a negative outlook on life. Whether his/her negativity is directed at a life change, a career situation, product enhancement, sales approach, or anything else, that negativity begets more negativity. Negativity deters success in any field or aspect of life. Of course, having a positive outlook in life is not always a natural and is sometimes difficult to maintain. However, with a little work and positive reinforcement, the benefits of getting rid of negative thinking patterns and actions, then developing positive thinking habits, will manifest themselves almost immediately. If you are negative, you attract the negative. If you are positive, you attract the positive. It's actually that simple.

Negative thought patterns don't build overnight, and they are usually rooted in reality. If your perception of your past, the things that have happened to you, is negative, your outlook will tend to be more negative. It will take a little bit of time to change your thought patterns. Thinking positive is a conscious lifestyle transformation, but it will change your results. Once you decide to weed out the negative and embrace change, you will be surprised by the transformation in your results. As you rid yourself of the negativity and build the positive, your confidence will grow. The more your confidence grows, the more positive you'll become, and the more you will see the benefits of this transformation in your life and career.

LEVERAGE YOUR UNIQUE SKILLS

Everyone is different. We all may have been all created equal, but our skill sets are very different. For me, sitting down and writing a book is pretty easy. I like doing it because I sincerely enjoy helping to make a positive difference in people's lives. Many people I run into say they would rather dig a ditch six feet deep by four feet wide, then fill it in and do it again before they would write a book. You have to stop long enough to know what you are skilled at doing. I know without us even meeting that you have at least a couple of unique skills that are better than others. Maybe you just take them for granted and don't realize you have them. What is your "superpower"? Sometimes it takes others to point these skills out to you, but you have to listen when they do.

HOW DO YOU DO THAT?

I personally find providing sales strategy to be extremely easy. After a short amount of time, I can find skipped steps and gaps in the sales cycle. It seems easy to identify the gaps in the sales cycle and offer ways to fill in what is missing so the salesperson has the best chance to win the business. Honestly, I never thought much about this apparent skill. One day I was sitting in a deal review session with people I thought were equal or better than I was at doing this. At the meeting was the CEO, President, VP of Sales, regional manager, and the sales rep. They went through all the details of how they had been pursuing a large opportunity. I listened intently, and after about twenty minutes, I offered suggestion after suggestion. The room went silent, and everyone just stared at me, which was uncomfortable until the CEO spoke up. "How did you do that?" he asked. I had no idea what he was asking. He then said, "I have never seen someone analyze an opportunity so quickly and precisely. You are 100 percent correct. We didn't see any of that." It was then I realized I had a unique skill and leverage it.

I leveraged this skill. As one example, a group inside of SAP regularly held QPQ deal review strategies sessions. They credited these sessions for adding $40 million in new business to their top line. SAP's VP felt they would have not won the business without these sessions. Brad Cates, former President of Standard Register Healthcare, credited $12 million of business won to the sales approach and QPQ deal review sessions. The point here is we all have some unique skills or "Super Powers". We have to recognize what these are and then apply them, if we are going to succeed at the highest levels.

It's wonderful to have unique skills, but if you don't use them and leverage your talents, then what's the value? I have a close friend who is a successful businessman and is by far the best networker I have ever seen. He is a true connector. He will know everyone in the room in a matter of minutes and quickly find something in common with them. Without exception, he can find someone they know in common. I am very impressed with his skill because it is not one of mine. When we were talking the other day, I pointed out to him that he is not leveraging that skill to move his business forward or achieve his goals. He pushed back a bit when I pointed it out, but after a few minutes, he agreed. It's just who he is, and he never thought much about it. Identify and leverage your unique skills, and you will transform your results.

GOOD IS THE EVIL TO GREAT

In the book *Good to Great* by Jim Collins, he explains how good companies, mediocre companies, and even bad companies can achieve enduring greatness. My question for you is, "What do you think 'good is the evil to great' means from an individual standpoint?

When it comes to results, when is good ever even good? *Never!* Good means you are better than most, but not great. Good to me is just above average. Keep in mind, "When you are average you are just as close to the bottom as you are to the top!" as basketball coach John Wooden writes in *A Lifetime of Observations and Reflections on and off the Court.*

Whether you are a sales professional or in an organization with the goal to grow, good is not good enough. We have to constantly change and transform if we are going to realize our full potential. If you don't, you simply become complacent and build a comfort zone for yourself. The company I profiled for you earlier was in a comfort zone with its price of $2,350. That price was in the company's comfort zone so it was very reluctant to change it. Words like "complacent," "comfort zone," and "average" are the kiss of death for any salesperson. I will say those words are the kiss of death for any organization too. To help you determine if you are making changes or not, below is a chart with a set of seven basic questions. I will challenge you to read these questions every Monday morning. It will only take you a couple of seconds to read these and reflect on where you are with regard to change.

- **What did you do differently from last week?**
- **What consistent changes are you making?**
- **What have you changed your opinion about?**
- **What specific actions have you taken to execute change?**
- **What will you focus on changing today?**
- **Have you had any new ideas?**
- **Have you acted on them?**

The bottom line is this: If you can't embrace change, you can't transform the results you need and want. Without change you probably are not going to try a completely different and new sales approach like QPQ, and you might not maximize your potential in any aspect of your life. As playwright George Bernard Shaw once said, "People are always blaming their circumstances for what they are. I do not believe in circumstances. The people who get on in this world are the people who get up and look for circumstances they want, and if they cannot find them, they make them." Don't wait for change to happen; be the catalyst and create positive change in your life, starting right now.

CHAPTER 2

TRANSFORMING YOUR SALES APPROACH—QPQ

M any people don't understand the role of the sales representative. Even the companies that hire sales reps often feel that the services or products the company provides are so superior to the rest of the market that they sell themselves. Many companies make the mistake of providing lots of product knowledge, but very little ongoing sales training. They seem to think that their products are so advanced that all reps need to do is show them to prospects and the prospects will immediately buy them.

In real life, it's extremely rare that a product/solution is so outstanding that it sells itself. Even if that circumstance did exist, it wouldn't last long. Why? Because there's always a competitor closing in on any successful new product, idea, service, or technological development.

For this reason, sales reps are often considered order takers or just a necessary evil. However, the record needs to be set straight. *The function of the sales rep is to get and keep new customers.* Without these new customers, a company will not grow; if a company isn't growing and moving forward, then it's falling behind, and its chances of surviving are bleak. Sales reps are critical to a company's success; they are the backbone of the organization.

Successful companies understand the value of each employee in the organization, especially salespeople. If an organization is going to grow and thrive, the investment made to help sales reps succeed should be increased annually.

In this economy, there is no time or investor patience for a "make it up as you go along" sales approach. The attitude some company executives have about investing in their sales organizations is always somewhat surprising to me. They want to wait until the market is better, their revenues pick up, or they have more money in the budget. Again, isn't that the definition of insanity? They are not willing to consider change, and they keep doing the same things without producing the desired results.

YOUR CHANCE TO EXCEL

Obviously, if you're reading this book, you're not one of those people who settle for the old worn-out excuses. You want to improve and transform. Fortunately, as a salesperson, it's easy to quantify the job you are doing.

As you strive to grow and develop an increasingly successful sales approach, it's essential that you understand the most effective ways to sell every opportunity. *Good salespeople personify the entrepreneurial spirit in all aspects of their day-to-day activities.* They need to have the mindset that they are working for themselves. In some commission-only compensation arrangements, it's as if you are running your own franchise. The company you represent is just the conduit to your success.

The best sales reps have a definite mindset that produces their outstanding results. Although they work within the boundaries set by the organization, they actually work for themselves. This is no different than a franchise owner. Every franchise has to comply with the corporate policy. Owners need to meet certain requirements/production criteria to keep their franchises. Sales is no different; you usually have to meet your quota to keep your job. Less-successful salespeople forget they are working for themselves. To be successful, you've got to run your territory as if it were your own business. If you were spending your own money for out-of-town sales calls, if you had to pay for literature, if you were charged for each lead and phone call, then you'd probably manage your time and prospects much differently. Develop a franchise mindset and the appropriate understanding of the role and responsibilities of your job. When you conduct yourself as a business owner, then you will get the most out of your franchise and be well on your way to success.

SELLING WITH YOUR BACKBONE—QPQ

Most people understand every sales pursuit is different. There are different issues, different personalities, and different circumstances. However, you still have to have a consistent sales approach. As a salesperson, wouldn't you like to have more control over your sales pursuits? As a salesperson, is it even possible to take control of your sales pursuits? The answer without a doubt is yes. Unfortunately, I find most salespeople allow the prospect to control what goes on in a sales pursuit. Most salespeople are in a *subservient position* with their prospects. They empower the prospect to set the tone and make up all the rules for the sales pursuit. If I said most salespeople are the puppets of their prospects, would you disagree? What if I went further and suggested that decision makers act like the puppet masters, and sellers allow them to pull all the strings? To paraphrase Peter Finch in the movie *Network*, hopefully, "You're mad as hell, and you aren't going to take it anymore!"

QPQ stands for *quid pro quo*. This is a Latin term that means "something for something." In translation, it means something in exchange for something of equal or greater value. If you are going to take some control and not be subservient to your prospects and clients, you have to establish a QPQ relationship, one based on mutual respect.

CONTROL

- **I don't have the confidence to stand my ground and dictate the rules of engagement.**
- **I fear rejection.**
- **The prospect might not like me.**
- **"The Golden Rule": He who has the gold makes the rules.**
- **I don't feel empowered to change the dynamic and take control.**
- **I don't know how to establish a QPQ relationship.**
- **I'm in sales, so my job is to serve.**
- *You can't say No to a prospect.*

If you want more control, why aren't you taking it? If you don't like being subservient, why aren't you changing that dynamic? Through hundreds of QPQ workshops around the world, when those questions are asked, we hear the common answers:

Have you ever bought into any of these bullet points? If you have, then you have put self-imposed restrictions on your ability to succeed. I'll explain how each one of these thought processes is wrong and can be turned around when we get deeper into the QPQ approach. First, let's visit some of the common mistakes when it comes to taking control in a sales cycle.

- **Selling to the wrong person**—Having a QPQ relationship or control with someone who doesn't make the decision will not help you and will elongate your sales cycle.

- **Not asking for something**—Prospects and clients ask salespeople for things all the time. They ask for proposals, meetings, RFPs to be filled out, and presentations. Rarely do I hear about salespeople asking for something or anything of real value in return for all they give.

- **Fear of alienating the prospect**—One of the oldest pieces of conventional sales wisdom is, people buy from people they like. If you buy into that thinking, you will be more concerned than you need to be about alienating the prospect. I challenge that wisdom and will offer you this: *People buy more from people they respect and trust.* Typically, if someone trusts you and respects you, they tend to end up liking you too. Make sure you have those in the right order and do not try so hard to get people to like you first.

- **Assuming too much**—The longer a person has been doing something, the easier it is to assume he/she knows the situation, buying cycle, issues, questions, and solution. They tend to accept the situation and rarely attempt to alter the course of the sales cycle.

- **Not asking open and direct questions**— Sometimes we don't ask questions because we are afraid of the answers. If we do this, then the prospect will always have control, and we'll be groping in the dark on how to best proceed.

- **Not enough homework upfront**—You have to do some work to determine who, when, and how to push a certain sales situation. Often, just too much is left uncovered, and there is a reluctance to take control.

- **Not setting the right expectations**—It's important to set the tone and work with the prospect to explain what you will do, what you won't do, and what you expect from him/her. This will quickly determine if this person will work with you or just wants you to be a puppet for him/her. *The main objective of QPQ is to establish a relationship based on mutual respect, give you more control over sales pursuits, and create collaboration in all aspects of the sales pursuit.* When you have all three of these, you tend to win the business. When you don't, you typically don't win, or the deal just stalls with no decision.

If the Transformational QPQ Sales approach is executed correctly, there is a collaborative relationship established with prospects and clients without confrontation. Let me recount a situation I experienced with Georgia Pacific.

GEORGIA PACIFIC'S EXPECTATIONS

I was selling to Georgia Pacific, which is a Fortune 50 company that is based in Atlanta. GP is one of the largest suppliers of paper products in the world. Like most very large organizations, it is used to dictating the terms and price for everything it wants to buy.

Smaller companies often think that having large, prestigious companies use their products gives their solution/product instant credibility. If a company like Georgia Pacific has purchased your solution, then it must be outstanding. It's natural for large companies to exploit this type of thinking and expect deeply discounted prices.

At the time, I was selling financial application/ accounting software. As with most robust software packages, our company had developed a graphical user interface (GUI) to go in front of the accounting software. The GUI gave the software the Windows look, which made it easy to use.

We didn't sell the GUI as a separate product, but GP wanted to buy the interface. In the middle of our presentation, GP's CIO asked the founder of our company what it would cost for them to purchase the GUI. Even though I've always believed, "Everything I have is for sale; we just need to agree on price," I was totally surprised when the founder replied, "You'll have to work that out with Bob."

Talk about being thrown a hot potato! We'd hardly even discussed this. I quickly went into my questioning mode. "Do you have a budget for the development of a GUI?" "How much do you feel it would cost you to develop something like this?" "Is time an issue for you?" "What are your alternatives?" I asked a few more questions, but the GP CIO wasn't helping me out much. Though I panicked inside, I collected myself and said, "$700,000."

GP's CIO said the price was too high, and the presentation continued. (Most large companies will always tell you that your price is too high. I could've said $10, and I would've gotten the same response.)

After the presentation, GP's CIO showed his hand a bit by continuing to express interest in the GUI. He let me know it wasn't in their budget, but they liked the product. He started to sell me on why it would be good for our company if GP adopted the use of the GUI. There was no way that I was going to give it to them. We weren't even looking to sell it at any price. I professionally told GP that giving the GUI away was not an option we could consider, and perhaps we should talk again if they found some money in their budget. They said they'd look into pulling some money out of other budgets, and they still wanted to evaluate the GUI. Their research teams looked at the product for about a week, which did not require much, if any, of my time. Ultimately, they wanted to use our GUI for all the software applications they developed in-house.

Remember, there is a sale made on every call. Either the prospects are selling you on what they need or want, or you are selling them on what you will and won't do.

The CIO and Georgia Pacific's corporate attorney invited me to a meeting to discuss how they could acquire this product. Having been involved with a few of these meetings in the past, I had a pretty solid idea of what to expect. This time they caught me off guard.

The three of us met in their palatial offices. In a company like GP, the CIO has a lot of decision-making power and deals with multimillion-dollar budgets, and he/she is usually never accessible to outside sales reps. Without exception, CIOs expect to get their way. As I sat down, the CIO said, "Like I told you a few weeks ago, we don't have any money budgeted for this product, so we need you to give us the use of the GUI for free." He went on to explain that GP was an IBM showcase account. People from all over the world came to GP to see what it was using before they made their own buying decisions. As he was trying to sell me on why I should give him the GUI for free, I did a quick calculation on what my commission was on *free*. You can probably guess what that was. Not realizing it, I made the mistake of rolling my eyes at his ongoing pitch for free software.

The CIO yelled at me in a way that my father never did when I was a kid. Since my father was a constant yeller, you can only imagine how loud the CIO was. "Who do you think you are? I told you, we had no budget for this! You had better wipe that look off your face! We can give you more business than your company can imagine, and I don't need your attitude," he yelled. He said a few other things, but you get the idea. I guess my feelings were written all over my face: $0 x 0 commission = $0 to pay my bills.

At this point, I hadn't said a single word in the meeting.

This was an interesting way to learn that I do tend to roll my eyes at things I think are ridiculous. Anyway, after the CIO was done trying to intimidate me, I looked him right in the eyes and said, "I'm sorry you feel that way, and I meant no disrespect with whatever facial expression I made, but I told you the price months ago. I also told you we were not going to give away the product. So this meeting is over. Please call me when you get some funds." I closed my notebook and stood up.

My response was just as shocking to him as his outburst was to me. Just as my hand touched the doorknob, he asked me to stay and see if we could work it out. The result was Georgia Pacific paid $700,000 for the product and received no discount.

By setting the expectation right up front, I earned the right to hold my ground on the price if they wanted the product. Now, $700,000 x X commission = $Y, and $Y is good!

The only time to give a discount is when you get something back from the prospect other than just a signed agreement. If you don't hold your ground, you're signaling the prospect that it's OK to walk all over you. Instead, you might say, "I'll lower my price in exchange for three personal referrals from your network." In this case, the prospects feel they are getting a deal because they are helping you. You end up making progress with your prospect, and you get three good contacts. In addition, you've saved face with the prospect by getting something in return for a discount on your product or service. You haven't devalued your product/service, and the prospect gets a lower price. Everyone wins in this situation.

QPQ

As mentioned earlier, the lynchpin of QPQ is getting something of equal or greater value when a prospect or client asks you for something. You have to know what you want, though. When we review this in our workshops, most of the time the exchange is not equal or greater. We find salespeople offering to do more work for a prospect than they should. "Equal or greater value" are the operative words. As a professional salesperson, you should expect something other than just a yes or no at the end of a sales cycle. What often happens, though? You go through months of calls, meetings, pricing, presentations, and the prospect lets you know at the end if you have won or lost. It is a big secret until the very end. The prospect has made up all the rules, and then you find out after all your hard work, time, and investment whether you have won or lost.

TEXAS HOLD 'EM

I want you to think about the situation that tends to repeat itself over and over again, like playing in a Texas hold 'em poker tournament. Texas hold 'em poker is one of the fastest-growing and most popular games in the world today. There are neighborhood games going on every night of the week. You can hardly turn on the TV without watching someone win a six- or seven-figure poker tournament.

I want to play poker with you. If I come to your company to teach the QPQ sales approach, I want you to set up a game of poker. I am there overnight, because the class is one and a half to two days long, so this will be perfect. Get as many other people as you can to join us. The bigger the game, the more money can be won. I will let you set the stakes, but the higher the stakes, the better. Any amount is OK with me. There is just one caveat: I get to make up the rules. I will let you know as we go along if we are playing high cards win or low cards win, and if there are any cards that are wild. Naturally, this will be based on what cards I get dealt.

I have yet to find anyone who will play in my poker game. I am a decent guy and will let you win a pot or two. But you would have to be a fool to play in this type of game. Let this poker game sink into your brain a bit. OK, now that you are sure you won't play, think about your sales pursuits. *Doesn't this poker game describe what typically goes on in your sales pursuits?* The prospect is controlling the game, often making up the rules as the pursuit goes along. You continue to throw your money and time into the pot, and then he/she lets you know at the end if you won or lost.

If you wouldn't play in my poker game with these rules, then don't play in a game that prospects often set up. They are essentially running the same type of game. The stakes are too high, and there is too much opportunity for you to lose. Don't get involved in pursuits that leave all chance of winning to someone else.

RELATIONSHIP SELLING

Another age-old saying in the school of conventional sales wisdom is, "Selling is about relationships." I happen to agree with this concept. What is missing in this statement is the definition of what kind of relationships. Think of any positive relationships in your life. They can be with friends, family, clients, anyone. What is a common denominator every good relationship has? There are a few, but one for sure is that there's a give-and-take aspect to it. You wouldn't have someone over to your house eight times who won't even return your calls. Why do so many sellers allow prospects to have a different standard from any other person in their lives when it comes to relationships? Is relationship selling defined as "the prospect gets to run over the salesperson, back up the truck, and do it again, and the salesperson just has to say, 'Thank you, sir, may I have another?'" What kind of relationship is that?

PROFESSIONALLY ASSERTIVE

In any other aspect of your life outside of business, if someone were treating you the way I described above, you would likely say something to him/her about how you feel. You should do that in business too. The great and powerful Oz is only a myth. The person you are selling to puts his/her pants on just like you. Eleanor Roosevelt said, "No one can make you feel inferior without your consent." It's OK to share how you feel with clients and prospects. We are all human.

I want to introduce the term "professionally asser-tive." You want to share your feelings, but you have to be professional and reasonable about it. We have all worked with some difficult people. That doesn't mean you can tell someone you think he/she is difficult. That is assertive, but it crosses the line into being unprofessional. It would have been reasonable and assertive if I had said what was really going through my mind to the Georgia Pacific CIO. I stopped and calculated what I thought my commission would be if I had done that. I refrained, as you know. I was professionally assertive and shared my feelings with him. Don't be afraid to let someone know how you feel, especially when they don't return your calls, don't reply to emails, or are hard to work with. You have absolutely nothing to lose.

CHAPTER 3

APPLYING TRANSFORMATIONAL QPQ

In so many words, Chapter 2 informed you that the prospect is not the king, or queen as it may be. Hopefully, you are starting to think hard about who's in control in your current sales pursuits. The old school taught us all that customers and prospects are always king. This means that the customer is always right. He/she is in control. If you are persistent enough, suck up enough, and lower your price enough, he/she will eventually buy from you.

The more service you offer a prospect, the better chance you'll have of winning the business.

The QPQ approach is totally opposed to subservient thinking and selling. The prospect is not king or queen. You are. You need to control all aspects of the sales cycle. Reps who bend over backwards to please everyone soon weaken their spines.

There are two reasons why you should always be in control of every selling situation:

1) Your income is dependent upon your sales volume.

2) You only have x amount of time to generate that volume.

Let's look at the first reason. If you're like most salespeople, you earn a percentage of your income from commissions. Most compensation plans are set up so that sales reps earn around 50 percent to 85 percent of their income from commission. The sales volume you produce directly influences the amount of money you earn for the year. I'm always amazed at how many sales reps seem to forget this fact. They seem to be content with letting the prospect be king and control the selling situation. They seem to be content with earning far less than they could.

The second reason why you should always control every selling cycle is that you have only a specific and limited amount of time to sell each day, each week, and each year. Time is the most valuable asset a salesperson has. You just don't have the time to hope a prospect is going to buy. You don't have the time or money to waste pursuing unqualified opportunities. How you spend your limited amount of time greatly affects your success in sales. Sellers need to manage their valuable time in a way that benefits their efforts and supports their goals.

PROFESSIONAL EVALUATORS

One of the hard lessons I learned early in my sales career was that some companies employ what I'll call, "professional evaluators." These evaluators apparently have nothing better to do than go to lunch with sales reps, have meetings with sales reps, accept perks from sales reps, but unfortunately, they never buy. They are time eaters. They always make you feel good about their intentions and usually express how much they like you, but they never can buy for one reason or another.

Those sales reps who fall into the trap set by professional evaluators become what I call, "paid tourists." These reps make trip after trip pursuing a prospect, yet they never bring home a signed contract. As long as you don't need to make money and your company is willing to support your nonproductive travels, then I guess it's OK to be a paid tourist. However, in today's economy, very few companies will put up with reps who don't produce. If you're going to travel, make sure that the trip will strongly enhance your chances for success. My advice is to make sure the return is worth the time spent.

WHY?

"Why?" is always a good and reasonable question to ask. Have you been around a three-year-old lately? Everything is, "Why, Mommy? or Why, Daddy?" They question everything. The first phase of QPQ is to simply ask your prospects why. Why are they asking for what they are asking for, whenever they are asking for something? How are they going to use it? Put your prospects in a position to sell you. Even if you know exactly why they are asking for a meeting, some more information, a demo—whatever it is—ask the question why.

I will promise you one of two things will happen every time you ask why:

A. After a little discussion, you will collaborate with your prospect and determine he/she doesn't need what he/she is asking for. Sometimes prospects don't even know why they asked. They asked because they have always asked for X. When you figure out they don't need what they asked for, you have now shortened your sales cycle and eliminated some unproductive work. Everyone needs shorter sales cycles. The longer a sales cycle, the better the chance something is going to go wrong.

B. What will likely happen is prospects will go into a big dissertation. They will explain in detail why what they need is very important and a critical aspect of their evaluation. They will be selling you aggressively on why they need what they are asking for. When this happens, just let them keep talking. The more value they put on what they are asking for, the better for you. The reason is simple. Do you recall the definition of QPQ? Something in exchange for something of equal or greater value. The more value they put on what they want, the bigger thing you can ask for in return, which sets us up for phase two of QPQ.

HELP ME HELP YOU

One of the key aspects of the Transformational QPQ Sales approach is getting prospects to help the sales rep help them. I've been asking prospects for years to "help me help you." When I heard Tom Cruise say that in the movie *Jerry Maguire,* I about fell out of my seat. I had been saying that for years!

GAINING CONTROL

Once prospects are helping you help them, it's important to remember that you're the one controlling the sales cycle. Once they have asked for something and placed a high value on it, you are now in the position to set some ground rules by setting up an exchange. At a minimum, the key points are that you want the prospect to do the following:

1. Grant you access to the people you need to work with.
2. Share his/her situation and issues with you fully.
3. Share his/her concerns about your offering.
4. Accept responsibility for his/her business issues.

5. Work with you to decide if it is possible to solve his/her challenges.
6. Commit to change and confirm that the status quo is not a likely option.
7. Agree to explore your offering as a potential solution.
8. Share his/her decision criteria.
9. Agree to a reasonable evaluation plan.

QPQ RIGHT UPFRONT

Asking the "why" question will set you up for a much different sales dynamic than you are probably experiencing. You also want to set up realistic timeframes for accomplishing the above points.

Points one, two, and three start immediately from your initial conversation with the prospect, and instantly when he/she asks you for anything. One through three must be established before a qualified sales cycle exists and you invest much time in pursuing the opportunity. Even before your sales cycle begins, you need to establish QPQ as part of the relationship right upfront. As one of a thousand examples, there is no sense in sending information/literature to a prospect if you cannot agree to set a follow-up appointment. You want to ensure the literature has been read and the prospect is ready to discuss the merits of what you sent to him/her. If he/she is vague or noncommittal, then don't waste your time. The prospect is unlikely to spend the required amount of time to make an informed decision to better his/her situation. This is an area in which reps do not establish control. Reps should set the proper tone for the entire sales cycle.

Another problem area is the timing of the presentation. There is no sense in performing a presentation unless

A. There is a reasonable buying timeframe established.

B. The decision maker is going to be involved.

C. There is a sense of urgency.

D. There is a defined need you can meet.

The opportunity should be fully qualified, and the prospect should be ready to make a buying decision. I work with reps daily who do not follow these simple criteria. Without exception, it comes back to bite them in the end. Either they have to do way more work, or their sales cycle suddenly stalls and they cannot figure out why.

If you can't establish a give-and-take relationship that enables you to set up reasonable timeframes for the sales cycle, then drop the prospect and find one who is more reasonable. It is almost impossible to do business with unreasonable prospects who have unrealistic expectations or demands. You should have a good idea how long is reasonable for the product or services you are selling.

THE EXCHANGE

You have set up the prospect perfectly with your "why" question. Now it is time for you to get something of equal or greater value. The exchange is the second phase in Transformational QPQ Selling. I have already given you one example, when the prospect asked you for information/literature. What we wanted in exchange was to set a time on the calendar to have a follow-up call. This is much better than chasing someone for weeks whom you had a good call with and sent some information to, only to find he/she is missing in action. Your contacts will be pleasantly surprised when you differentiate yourself from the pack by establishing a reasonable give-and-take relationship right from the first call. Why? Because there are so many average salespeople in the market who don't establish any kind of a relationship at all and allow prospects to run them around.

DILBERT

Another example of a good QPQ exchange comes when it's time for a meeting. The prospect wants you to come to him/her and have a discussion. Let's assume you have to buy an airplane ticket, rent a car, and take an entire day to go to this meeting. What do you think would be a reasonable exchange? Most of the time, a good and valuable exchange would be to meet with the decision maker. It doesn't matter if it is the first meeting or not. He/she is asking you to spend a lot of time and money to attend a meeting. In theory, you are calling on this organization because you can help it in some way. It is more than reasonable to expect the decision maker to spend an hour with you to explore how your offering can help him/her. If he/she won't do that, you have to ask yourself, "Is he/she a qualified prospect?" Can you afford to attend this meeting? Many salespeople think just the opposite of this, and they feel lucky to have been granted the meeting at all. Two questions come to mind with this thinking. First, how many sales pursuits happen year after year with no fruit for your labor? You might not lose the business, but the prospect just stays with his/her current solution—status quo. We find 50 percent to 80 percent of sales pursuits end up in this category for our clients before the start of one of our projects or classes with them. The other question is, "How many times do you find yourself having multiple meetings?" *Once "Dilbert" is convinced you are worthy, he will grant you access to the man behind the curtain.* "Dilbert" is a term we use for the person who poses as the decision maker, but has no real authority. We'll discuss Dilbert more in later chapters.

GOOD FOR THEM

QPQ is based on collaboration. It should not feel like a tit-for-tat exchange or "I will if you will." If QPQ is executed properly, the approach will not be confrontational. If a sales situation does become confrontational, you have to stop and determine why the prospect is acting in an unreasonable manner. Is he/she being unreasonable, or are you? Again, 99 percent of the time, especially after going through the QPQ class in detail, you will find out the prospect/client is being unreasonable.

Phase three of QPQ is designed to disarm any potential for confrontation so the prospect never experiences a tit-for-tat feeling.

Phase three of QPQ is simply selling the prospect on the fact that what you are asking for (QPQ phase two) is good for him/her. This is where your real selling skills come into play. Transformational QPQ Selling is a new approach that offers different tactics than sellers have been classically trained for. It is a much different way to approach sales pursuits and interact with prospects for most salespeople. A lot of practice and a deeper understanding might be required before you jump right into applying QPQ. Certainly this phase requires some planning and practice so it comes off naturally and in a conversational style.

MEETING EXCHANGE

In the example presented previously, in QPQ phase one the prospect asked for a meeting. The prospect went to great lengths explaining why they felt the meeting was important. Our QPQ exchange is that we want to meet with the decision maker along with the person with whom we have been interacting; this is QPQ phase two. Without stopping or hesitating, we move right into phase three of QPQ. Sell the person you are talking to on the reasons why it would be good for them to have the decision maker at the meeting. "I really need to have (the decision maker—name and/or title) at our meeting.

It will be good for you to get their involvement so you don't have to explain everything we went over at a later time. You might get asked some questions at a later date that you don't know the answers to. Also, if we get them involved now, they might get excited about the project, and we can start helping you sooner rather than later." There are many different talk tracks to phase three of QPQ. You have to think through them and make sure you are always keeping the prospect's best interest in mind.

THE STRATEGIC WITHDRAWAL

Regardless of how big the commission potential is, you have to have a predetermined point at which you are willing to walk away from an opportunity. Or better, to walk away from what you thought might be an opportunity that is not one. It's good for the prospect to know what this point is also. You may have heard it is OK to fire customers. I know your pipeline is already a little light, and I am suggesting you fire prospects. Truly, I have not lost my mind. I do want you to fire the tire kickers who won't work with you and aren't going to buy. I hope this doesn't represent your pipeline of prospects.

The strategic withdrawal is one of the most powerful and underutilized sales strategies you can employ.

There are so many examples I could use to illustrate why the strategic withdrawal works. Let's travel all the way back to the Garden of Eden. Adam could have had *any* fruit in the garden but one, the apple. What is the one he craved the most? The apple. As soon as you tell a person he can't have something, he seems to want it more.

WALKING AWAY

The reasons you might want to walk away and apply a strategic withdrawal are the following:

○ Provoke a response and see where you stand.

○ Move a prospect forward or out of your pipeline.

○ Change the dynamics of the sales cycle.

○ Get the time back and spend it finding a prospect who will buy from you.

• **Provoking a response:** If you withdraw from an evaluation, and the prospect doesn't respond or responds by saying, "Don't let the door hit you on the backside," then it is very unlikely he/she intended to buy from you in the first place. I would rather know that sooner than later. When I explain *how* to apply a strategic withdrawal, you will realize that you have nothing to lose. The objective is for the prospect to plead with you not to withdraw and then start working with you in a different manner.

• **Move a prospect forward or out of your pipeline:** Every salesperson reading this has "deadwood" in his/her pipeline. Some prospects stay in the pipeline for years. By applying a strategic withdrawal, you will either move them forward and get something going, or move them out of your pipeline. It does a salesperson no good to fool himself/herself or anybody else about how big his/her pipeline is when it is full of moldy deadwood.

- **Transforming the dynamics of the sales cycle:** When your access is getting blocked from the decision maker, when prospects make commitments they don't keep, when dates seem to always slip, and when your phone calls go days without being returned, it's time to transform the dynamics of the sales cycle. Life is too short to be disrespected by people who want to play the "sales evaluation game." Something has to change if you are reasonably going to get control of the sales pursuit and win the business. How many times have you seen the above behavior all the way through a sales cycle and then won the business? I am going to go out on a limb and guess not too often. That being the case, let's make some changes and transform these types of pursuits.

- **Get the time back and spend it finding a prospect who will work with you:** I understand it is much easier to pursue a "definite possible maybe" prospect vs. prospecting to find another more qualified opportunity. Refer back to your change chart in Chapter 1 and measure how much pursuing "definite possible maybe" prospects is moving you forward and closer to your goals.

WHEN TO APPLY THE STRATEGIC WITHDRAWAL

As an outside consultant, the vision of when to apply the strategic withdraw is crystal clear. When you are in the forest and the trees seem to be closing in on you, it is more difficult to see clearly. When you hesitate to apply this strategy, refer to my poker game offer and the statistic of how many of your sales pursuits end up with no fruit. The time to apply the strategic withdrawal is when there is none of the following:

- **Respect**
- **QPQ exchanges**
- **Collaboration**
- **Access to the people you need to meet with**
- **Commitment to move forward**
- **Urgency**
- **There is limited information given**
- **There is a bias against you or for someone else.**

HOW TO APPLY THE STRATEGIC WITHDRAWAL

To apply the strategic withdrawal, you have to address the main decision maker. I understand the argument from my many years in the software business that there are often many decision makers. I find this almost never to be the case. There are always a lot of influencers to the decision, but at the end of the day, there is always one decision maker.

The decision maker is someone who could make the decision if he/she wanted to without the input of anyone else.

You might not have reached the decision maker nor have a relationship with them, and is one of the reasons you are strategically withdrawing.

You want to strategically withdraw in this order:

A. In person
B. In a letter
C. By email

Withdrawing in person gives you the opportunity to explain your case, your feelings, and the well-thought-out decision not to pursue their business. You can have some back and forth with a face-to-face meeting. Then you can decide to finally withdraw on the spot, or get the prospect to commit to change a few things.

Withdrawing in a letter gives you the best chance to get your message read. You recall what a letter is, right? The thing you put a stamp on and put in the mailbox. An old-school approach, I know. Emails are often rerouted, lost, or never read. Hand-addressed envelopes are almost always opened.

Don't fall into the trap of trying to sell in this letter. Keep the letter simple. It has to be absolutely accurate with the facts that solidified your decision to withdraw. You are letting the decision maker know you don't see anything changing and that you are withdrawing from consideration. You will want to give the decision maker an opening to call you or respond in some way if they are interested in changing the situation.

Should you inform Dilbert you are going to be sending his boss or his boss's boss a letter withdrawing from consideration? Not a chance, until you are sure whomever you sent the letter to has already read it. If Dilbert knows beforehand, they will sabotage you. He or she will put a spin on your withdrawal so as not to reflect on his or her actions in a negative light. He or she will say something like, "We decided the Transition-Group was too expensive, so we eliminated it from consideration. Be on the lookout for some sour-grapes letter they will send whining about our decision." You don't want to be beat by Dilbert!

Email is my least preferred way to withdraw, but sometimes it's your only option. If, for some reason, you can't use the US Postal Service, your email should be crafted exactly like your written letter. There is always the option of sending both the letter and an email.

OBJECTIONS—PHASE FOUR OF QPQ

Applying Transition QPQ is new to you, and it will certainly be new to your prospects. They are used to getting what they want, when they want it. Be prepared for the objections you will get. There is some good news here, though. There will be only four objections you are likely to hear when applying QPQ.

- "It's our policy to do…"
- "If I do that for you, I have to do it for everyone."
- "No one else is asking me for this."
- "I want you to work with our process."

Here are the QPQ phase-four objections:

"It's our policy to do…": For now and evermore when you hear that, I want you to reply, with a straight face, "Our company policy is… (the exact opposite of what they said theirs was). Can we find a way to work around these two policies?" Who said the prospect's company's policy trumps your company policy? You will learn pretty quickly if you can find some common ground and work together.

"If I do that for you, then I have to do it for everyone." My first question is, "Why do they feel that way?" You should persuade them they don't have to do the same for everyone, especially if the other competitors aren't asking for whatever you suggested. Take an even playing field if you have to. Your objective is to put your best foot forward and have your day in court.

"No one else is asking me for this": This objection is probably the best opportunity you will have to sell. You will often get responses two and three combined ("No one else is asking for this. Plus, if I do that for you, then I have to do it for everyone"). If you get this objection, it is a perfect opportunity to set up your competition without disparaging them. You can apply phase three of QPQ again, and this will significantly differentiate you from everyone else.

SHIPXACT INC.

After a frustrating day of prospecting, my phone rang. When I answered it, the gentlemen on the other end said, "Bob, you were referred to me as an expert in transformation, sales strategies, and sales training. We are looking for consulting, training, and an organization to help us increase our revenues. How can you help us?" I almost fell out of my chair. Our referral network gave me an over-the-top endorsement. I was also informed by the referral partner exactly what this organization's issues were before he had called.

At this point, what would you have done? I think most salespeople would have started tossing out solutions. They would have told him exactly what they had to offer in each one of the areas he needed help with. I'll admit, it took everything I had not to elaborate on our expertise. That would have been premature and could have cost us the business.

I restrained myself. Instead, I asked him to tell me about his company and give me more detail. I wanted to know why he had a need, what was driving the need, what timeframes he had, and the cost expectations. I wanted to shoot off the shotgun, certain I would hit something based on his opening request. It was much more prudent to get *all* the answers to the selling test, so I could take aim before I shot.

The person on the other end of the phone was more than happy to share with me all the information I wanted. He went on for twenty to thirty minutes. Every word he spoke was like putting money in the bank. He was telling me everything I needed to know to satisfy him that we were the only alternative he could reasonably consider. With each word, the target got closer and more in focus. At this point, neither a shotgun nor a rifle was needed. I could take out a knife to carve out this opportunity.

Putting my enthusiasm on hold for thirty minutes made selling this opportunity much easier.

I was invited to dinner with the VP and president of the company. They announced we were one of three companies they had narrowed their search to. Their plan was to send out a small questionnaire to the finalists, evaluate the answers, and then make their decision. Here was a QPQ opportunity. They were asking me to fill out a small thirty-five-page questionnaire. Here is an example of all four phases of QPQ in action.

My first response was to ask why they felt the need to send out the questionnaire. They justified their need and the approach to send out the questionnaire. I told them I would be happy to fill out their questionnaire, and once they saw my responses their decision would become easier. What I suggested, instead of just mailing in the answers as they suggested, was that it would be good for them if we set up a time for me to present my answers in person. That way we could discuss if there were any exceptions to my answers, and I could share the philosophy behind each response. Did you recognize QPQ phases one, two, and three? They replied with, "The other vendors are not asking for that. Besides, if we do that for you, then we have to do it for them."

QPQ phase four. I said without hesitation, "I am surprised no one else is asking to do that. If they aren't even asking you to present in person, I'm not sure why you think you would have to give them that opportunity. I am willing to take my time, come back here, and sit with the team to go through every answer in detail. It is important you have as much information as possible to make an informed decision. If the other guys are just willing to mail in their answers, and that is the kind of attention you are getting before the sale, what kind of attention do you think you will get after you sign a contract with one of them?" They thought about it for a minute and agreed with me. As soon as they agreed, I had a huge advantage over the other competitors. To this day, I am sure the competitors don't even realize why they lost.

Perfecting and applying the four phases of Transformational QPQ Selling will transform your results in ways you can't imagine. Now that you have a good foundation, let me offer you some real case studies in Chapter 4. Think through what you would have done, given the same situations.

CHAPTER 4

TRANSFORMATIONAL QPQ SELLING CASE STUDIES

TRANSFORMING YOUR RESULTS

The best way to learn anything is to get out and try it. Also, hearing about specific cases where the approach was applied will drive home many of the points in the last chapter. The key to this chapter is to relate these actual sales pursuits to situations you have had in the past or are experiencing currently. Regardless of the case studies I have used in this book, keep in mind the Transformational QPQ Sales approach is universally accepted. We have had successful engagements world-wide with companies that range from selling corrugated boxes to engineering services to software. The key principles of the QPQ Sales approach are:

- Taking control of the sale cycle
- Establishing a respectful give-and-take relationship
- Collaboration throughout the engagement
- Be willing to walk away from opportunities that aren't going to buy from you
- Having courage and confidence when asking for Quid Pro Quo

In our QPQ workshops, it is always surprising how much courage and confidence is displayed when I ask what the group would do in certain situations. When we get deep into QPQ phases and apply them to real-life situations, the courage and confidence seems to dissipate. Let's see how you do.

3M CORPORATION

At one time in my career, I was a VP for a small, self-funded software company and was pretty comfortable in the saddle. We were growing but had limited resources. I had laid out guidelines for the sales force for the things we would and would not do in the course of pursuing business. During this period, 3M happened to be the forty-sixth largest company in America. Having 3M use our product would be a huge and highly marketable stamp of approval. Also, if 3M was a reference, it could bring millions of dollars to our bottom line.

This QPQ adventure started when one of our sales reps called to inform me 3M was very interested in our solution. He told me the company was looking for solutions for all of their nineteen international branches. He wanted me to travel with him to 3M headquarters to give a brief overview of our company's international strategy.

Considering we did not have an international strategy and did not have any installations outside North America, I was reluctant to waste my time on this call. To make matters worse, 3M had just signed a million-dollar agreement with a competitor for enterprise resource planning (ERP) software. This competitor had a worthy financial software offering that integrated perfectly with their ERP solution. This made me certain I was not interested in making a trip to Minnesota in February.

As you'll learn in the chapter on qualification, bold, direct questions can help you quickly determine if you have an opportunity or not. I made 3M leaders convince me they were seriously considering our solution. If you think there are compelling reasons why someone should not buy your product, you are probably right. In this case, 3M had already purchased the competitor's ERP solution, so they had an established relationship. The competitor had service personnel and offices in every country where 3M was looking to install the software. In addition, the competition was a much larger organization then we were. On our side, we had no international installations, no foreign offices, no ERP solution, and we were small. From my viewpoint, using the information I had at the time, I would have bought from the other guys. At least I was being true to the Transformation QPQ Selling dictum that you should be honest with yourself at all times.

However, further qualification brought out some very useful information. In this case, 3M planned to use the best breed software to meet their needs, and it wanted centralized support based out of Minneapolis. There was no question we could provide 3M with both the best software and customer support out of Minnesota.

After a lot more qualification and being "encouraged" by our founder/CEO, I decided to invest the time and make the call. Hey, it was 3M, after all.

So off I flew in the dead of winter to make a sales call. In college, for some strange reason, I had one of my classes in the medical school. Carved into the wooden desk by some frustrated soon-to-be doctor were the words, "Someone is going to pay for this." This is exactly what was running through my mind the entire flight. Fortunately, prior to my trip, the founder of the company and I had done a little preparation on the international plan. Keep in mind, nothing existed when we first got the call from 3M. When I got to Minnesota, all the 3M folks wanted to hear about was an hour of detail on our international plan.

As it turned out, 3M was a good prospect, but our sales rep on the account hadn't done a particularly good job at qualifying. He didn't know the decision maker, what the timeframe was, the exact steps in the sales cycle, or the evaluation criteria. He didn't get to come home on the plane either. He had to stay in Minnesota until he had every answer to every question that was unasked and unanswered about this opportunity. Never again did he make the mistake of not being prepared.

One of the things he found out was that 3M was having a meeting in Singapore with nineteen of their executives. This meeting would be where the executives would select the software solution that they felt best met their needs. I received a call from the project leader, "Dilbert" (project leaders are almost always Dilberts), telling me they were having this meeting in Singapore. With less than ten days' notice, he needed us to be there for a three-hour presentation. Keep in mind, Singapore was a thirty-two-hour plane ride from Boston. So what do you think? Thirty-two hours on an airplane, halfway across the world, for a three-hour presentation, on the chance 3M might buy from us?

At this point, we'd never spoken with the decision maker, and all the other competitive issues still lingered in my head. How does that sound to you? Would you go in to the founder of the company and say, "I'm on my way to Singapore to chase this deal. It will only cost about $10,000 to pursue this opportunity." To make it a bit more compelling, the personal commission was $300,000, not to mention the status our company would get by signing 3M to nineteen international sites. You make the call. Are you going to make the trip? Are you going to put your neck on the line for a definite-possible-maybe opportunity? OK, it is 3M, and there is that $300,000 commission.

The correct response is, "Maybe."

First, though, there were conditions that needed to be met—QPQ exchanged. Remember what started this story? The Transformational QPQ Sales approach is not to ask, "How high?" whenever someone asks you to jump. Setting expectations and establishing a respectful give-and-take relationship is the foundation of the QPQ Sales approach. If you can't establish a give-and-take relationship, move on to someone who is interested in solving a problem and not playing a sales evaluation game. This approach will put off most prospects, but you just have to explain to them you're not interested in wasting their time or yours. Apply QPQ phase three.

The project leader I was dealing with was quite put off, despite my best efforts of walking him through all the QPQ phases. After all, he was from 3M, and he was offering me the opportunity for a huge sale. How dare I ask him a few hard, bold, direct questions? Well, I had definite reasons. I needed to understand why we'd get only three hours for our presentation. Also, I needed to feel I was on a level playing field with the competitor, from whom they'd just purchased the ERP software. Singapore was a long way, and if we didn't go, we were out of the evaluation. On the other hand, if we did go, I wanted to make sure we had a legitimate chance of winning. There was a lot of pressure. Go and win and you are a hero. Go to Singapore and lose for the reasons you think you are likely going to lose, and the founder will lose faith in your skills. He will also question your ability to make prudent business decisions.

The 3M project leader assured me each organization would get three hours, and only three hours, to make its presentation. He also assured me there was just us and one other competitor. At the end of this meeting, they would decide which package they felt served their needs the best. He went on to convince me it was a level playing field, too.

I wanted one more thing before I could commit to this journey across the world. Can you think what that might be? Has our QPQ exchange been of equal or greater value? All we have received is an opportunity to present and some answers to our concerns. Does that seem like an equal exchange for a thirty-two-hour plane ride halfway across the world to Singapore? If you think it is not, what would you ask for at this point?

I needed to meet the decision maker. Many reps feel they can sometimes skip this step. Why do you need to meet the decision maker when he/she has put a very capable and knowledgeable person in charge of the project (Dilbert)? The reason is straightforward: A project leader is not a salesperson or a decision maker. Don't make the mistake of letting your sponsor or main contact do the selling for you. Whether the presentation is to a board of directors or to the main contact's manager, you need to do your own selling. If project leaders (or others whom salespeople put their fates into the hands of) were good salespeople, they'd be doing that for a living instead of the job they have. It's very important to stay in control of the sales process. That is the cornerstone of the QPQ approach. As soon as you turn the selling over to anyone else, you've lost control. You've left your success to fate, or some other mystic force, hoping to get the sale.

In this case, there was no way I was going to fly halfway around the world and leave anything to fate. When I explained that I needed to meet with the decision maker, the project leader let me know why that was impossible.

Here is another example of "there is always a sale made on every call." Either you sell the prospect on providing you with what you need to know, or he/she sells you on why you can't have it. Be the better salesperson and don't back down if your requests are reasonable.

My request to have a meeting with the decision maker was very reasonable, especially considering what the company was asking me to do (give and take). The project leader told me in no uncertain terms this was not possible. I let him know we would not be attending his party in Singapore if that were the case. He explained that meant we were out of the deal. I understood. We hung up and left it at that.

What it really meant was no $300,000 commission check. It was a tough call, but if you're not going to get to play your best hand, there's no sense in wishing for a sale to close.

Amazing as it was, the next day I received another call from the project leader. He called to let me know that he had checked with the decision maker whom he refused to identify, and there was no way to meet with me. His boss was already in Singapore. He went on to let me know the decision maker held this meeting once a year, and it was the time he met with all his people from the nineteen other countries. Finally, when he stopped trying to sell me on why it was impossible to accommodate my request, he asked if I would now come to Singapore. It was 3M, a nineteen-country opportunity, and there was that $300,000 commission rolling around in my head. Again you make the call. Are you going or not?

My answer was, "No." As far as I was concerned, nothing had changed from the day before. What had happened was the project leader thought through his sales strategy and gave me another pitch. My response made him absolutely crazy. I proceeded to tell him again why I needed to meet with his boss. I asked, "Does he eat breakfast, lunch, and dinner?"

"Of course he does," the flustered project leader replied.

I said, "If the guy won't sit down with me for thirty minutes and discuss the project and our solution after the effort you are asking from me, then he won't buy from us." This is true more times than not, and you need to keep this in mind as you go through your sales cycle.

Again the project leader hung up, frustrated with my response. And again, I saw that $300,000 float right by me. About an hour later the project leader called me again; he was like a stalker now. I answered the phone, and all he said was, "OK"

Playing dumb, I said, "OK, what?"

"He'll meet with you."

I replied, "Who will meet with me?" The decision maker agreed to meet with me for breakfast after our presentation. I pushed hard to speak with him before I went, but I couldn't make that happen. So it was off to Singapore. In the spirit of complete disclosure, the Transformational QPQ Sales approach was not fully baked at the time; there was no email, Skype, and so on at the time either. If the exact same situation occurred today there would be a few more steps required before I got on that plane to Singapore.

The day I left there was so much snow on the runway in Boston the plane was fish tailing. After thirty-two hours and six movies, I arrived in Singapore. If you've ever made a trip like that, you know what real jet lag is all about. I slept for a day and a half. My colleague had to finally wake me up, or I might still be sleeping.

Our presentation was to begin at 7:00 p.m. on Thursday. Mind you, these 3M guys had been in meetings since Sunday, and they had been in the room we were presenting in since about 8:00 a.m. This project leader was not helping us out much, was he? I gave my PowerPoint presentation, sat in the back of the room, and let the consultants show our solution. On the desk in front of me was the agenda for the week. I casually flipped through it. I saw our slot at 7:00 p.m. on Thursday. When I flipped the page, there it was. My biggest fear had been realized. The competitor had the entire next day to present.

If you recall, the "level playing field" was three hours for each of us. You can only imagine how mad I was, especially at myself. I knew better, and yet there I was, sitting in Singapore, feeling like I had been put in a matrix for just comparison purposes with little chance to earn the business.

The rest of the night went well, and our presentation was excellent. Many of the 3M executives came up afterward to let us know how impressed they were with our solution. They had nothing to do with the agenda or any of the preplanning that the project leader and I had agreed to. The good news for us was that we were set for breakfast the next morning with the decision maker. How would you handle this breakfast meeting?

If you are ready to share your feelings in a profession-ally assertive way, you are right on track.

At this point, I felt we had nothing to lose. Our competitor was given the entire day to present. 3M had already invested in its ERP solution. The project leader wasn't helping us. Even though I knew we had the best solution, the cards were stacked against us. Breakfast with "the man" was our last hope.

It was time to take the gloves off. I was with one of the founders of the company, who was on the develop-ment side of the business. The plan was to play "good cop and bad cop." You've seen that done on every police show on TV. You get the suspect in the room. The bad cop threatens to kill him, while the good cop holds the bad cop off, trying to make peace. I got to be the bad cop and was pretty excited about it.

We all met for breakfast the next morning. The deci-sion maker was exactly what I expected. He was a gruff old guy who didn't want to be there and certainly was not too interested in me. When I said good morning, he grunted back. We all sat down at a very small table. Since there weren't going to be many pleasantries exchanged, I started right up. One of the guys from 3M made the mis-take of breaking the ice by asking, "How do you think it went last night?" That was all I needed to let loose.

"I'm glad you asked," I said. "I have to tell you I'm dis-appointed by 3M and its representatives. I'm pretty sure we don't want you as a customer. I know this is the project leader's first project, but you don't lie or treat a potential partner the way he's treated us." The project leader's face turned beet red as I continued. He would not look at me or speak to me. At one point, he asked my partner to make me stop saying these things. Finally, the decision maker had heard enough. He put down his fork and said, "I am sorry you had this experience. I will tell you, the feedback I got from your presentation last night was exceptional. You solved a few issues we've been trying to solve for years. Right now, I would say you guys are way ahead. I need you to do one more thing for us. Could you go to Mexico next month for one more presentation?"

What are you going to say to this? You don't get much time to think about it. Are you going to Mexico?

My response was direct, "Absolutely not! We came to Singapore on good faith and a promise of a level playing field. We have spent a lot of time and money to try to help you. You've seen enough information to make an informed decision. I know we can provide a solution that no one else can. We would love your business, but we were successful before we got here and will be successful when we leave."

Was I being unreasonable? All things considered, I hardly think so. I believe the decision maker respected the stance we took. He acknowledged what I said and expressed that he understood our position.

The outcome of this was the project leader was taken off the project and sent to the Netherlands. 3M signed a multimillion-dollar deal with us, with no discount. It gave us a great reference and a big press release and put us in nineteen countries.

The point of this 3M case study is the following: You've got to apply QPQ sincerely and reasonably. There is no point in sheepishly asking for something, not getting it, and then giving up to what they wanted anyway. As long as you are reasonable and have good logic in phase three of QPQ, you should hold firm to your requests.

In the case of 3M, if the sales activity was not controlled, we would've had a much longer sales cycle at best. At worst, we wouldn't have won the business. The longer the sales cycle, the more opportunity for negative things to creep in and prevent your sale from happening.

Do you think we would have won 3M's business if we had not met the decision maker? With 3M, we never asked for anything that was unreasonable. We always remained completely professional, yet assertive. We told the prospect no. Saying no when necessary was essential to winning the business. Too many sales reps don't have the courage or feel empowered enough to say no when it's needed. They feel they will lose their opportunity or upset the prospect in some way. It's very reasonable to say no as long as you are reasonable and professional in your approach.

YOU DON'T UNDERSTAND

One of many unique things about our Transformational QPQ classes is one of the first things we say to our clients:

"If you don't like what we are saying, don't buy into what we are telling you, or are just uncomfortable, please feel free to tell us." Indus had about ninety salespeople it wanted to train in the Transformational QPQ approach, so we broke it up into two classes. We had just completed explaining the QPQ phases, given a few examples, and done some casework in the QPQ workbook, when one of the reps raised his hand and told me QPQ was great, but I didn't understand. I asked him what I didn't understand, and this case study is what he told me.

INDUS AND THE SOUTHERN COMPANY

Bill was a new representative for Indus. Indus develops, licenses, implements, supports, and hosts service delivery management (SDM) solutions designed to help clients optimize customer management, assets, workforce, spare-parts inventory, tools, and documentation in order to maximize performance and customer satisfaction, while reducing operating expenses. The company's products have been licensed for use by more than four hundred companies in more than forty countries, representing diverse sets of industries. About a year before Bill started at Indus, the company acquired Wishbone Systems, Inc. The acquisition led to the formation of the company's service suite that forms a part of its SDM solutions. Indus substantially reworked the Wishbone product, making many changes and enhancements and got rid of any sign of the old Wishbone product.

Bill was calling on the current client base in his territory to introduce himself to the clients. One of these was the Southern Company. The Southern Company is a superregional energy company. Southern Company was ranked number 165 on the Fortune 500 listing of the largest US corporations.

Bill called the name provided to him on the list of client contacts. In this case, he called Steve, manager of systems. Does this sound like a decision maker's title for an opportunity of this magnitude? Steve explained Southern Company had purchased the Wishbone product for $13 million four years ago. The product had been a disaster for the company, and the people who selected the software were getting ready to throw it out and look for another solution. He knew that Indus had recently purchased Wishbone. Southern Company had tried for years to get the product to work for it, but failed. The new project for a solution will cost Southern Company about $25 million.

Can you figure out what mistake Bill has already made? He called Dilbert right out of the box. You should always start at the top and work your way down. By starting your pursuits high, your access is less likely to be blocked.

Bill was eager and hungry to build his pipeline, not to mention wanting to significantly increase his bank account. Bill began to sell Steve on the changes and benefits of working with Indus. Steve told Bill there was no way he was going to risk his career on looking at some reworked version of Wishbone. Bill now really started to sell, because this was a huge opportunity, the biggest of his life. He also knew all of the changes that had been made to the Wishbone product.

Even though Bill got excited and made a mistake, Steve asked Bill to send him literature and bullet point all the changes that had been made to the Wishbone product.

Understanding the Transformational QPQ Sales approach, what should Bill have done at this point?

Considering the circumstances, a lot of salespeople would consider it a victory that Steve was even willing to look at what Bill had put together. With the QPQ approach, we need more, though. The right thing to do was to get something in return for putting together a fact sheet pointing out the differences and enhancements to the Wishbone product. Bill wanted to meet with Steve in person and go over the changes.

Steve granted Bill's request. There was one wrinkle: He told Bill that he was only allowed in the lobby of the building just for a few minutes, and he didn't want to be seen talking to Bill because the internal politics around this issue were too hot. He would try to get some of his subordinates to look at Bill's literature and measure their interest level for him. Like most non-QPQ salespeople would feel, Bill was grateful for the opportunity and happily dropped off the information Steve asked for. Over a two-week period, Bill called Steve repeatedly to follow up on the information he provided him, with no success in reaching him.

Let's stop here and reread. Bill was only allowed in the lobby of the building. Seriously, what do you think the odds are that Southern Company was going to spend $25 million with Bill when he was not even allowed in the offices? If there is not some real QPQ exchanged, and this opportunity was not transformed in some way, then Bill had no chance. When Bill was telling this story, I asked him what he thought his chances of winning were, considering he was not allowed in the offices. He felt he had a 20 percent chance, his boss said 10 percent, and the VP of sales said 5 percent. OK, fair enough. The follow-up question was a little tougher for all of them. "How much time are you spending on pursuing this opportunity?" No one answered, but you can probably imagine they were spending way more time on this than the percentage chance of winning could justify.

Bill finally got hold of Steve six weeks later. Steve told Bill the next step was that they were sending out an RFP to seven vendors. The RFP was about forty pages long. He let Bill know he did a very good job of selling, and Steve got him on the list. He could make no promises to Bill, considering the history of Wishbone, but at least Bill would have a chance to fill out the RFP. Steve had been appointed project leader for finding a new solution to the Wishbone product. Bill had three weeks to get his response back to Steve. After that they would consider the alternatives and move to the next step. Steve was a little vague on the next step since this was his first project. He thought it would likely be a round of presentations.

How do you think Bill should be feeling at this point? Should Bill be grateful he was one of seven on the list? Do you think Bill has a one-in-seven chance of winning this business at this point? With your newfound mindset of applying QPQ, what would you want in return for filling out this RFP? You should want to be granted access to the offices first. But seriously, don't you want an audience with the decision maker to explain why the company bought the Wishbone product? You need to address the misconceived notions about the product and see if you can get a fair shot at this business.

How do you rate Steve as a "sponsor" or "champion"? Your answer should have been, "low." He had not granted Bill access to anyone else and kept giving Bill more work to do.

Bill filled out the RFP, then waited the three weeks Southern Company asked for to review all the responses. Bill called Steve again, and after about six calls without a response, Bill finally reached him. Steve apologized for not getting back to Bill, but he had been underwater with all the calls, reviewing the RFPs, and his daily routine. (Sound familiar?) Steve was excited to tell Bill that he was one of vendors they were going to invite in for a presentation. They only disqualified one vendor, so six different organizations would be presenting.

This now was starting to feel like sales-cycle water-boarding. How would you be feeling at this point? What do you think Steve's motivation was? Would you take the offer to present at this point? What would you *really* want if you were going to go ahead and present? What's a good QPQ exchange? List all the gaps in your sales cycles at this point.

Steve needed Bill to present so he could disqualify him. Steve had to be looking for reasons not to buy from Bill all along. Bill had not moved beyond Steve in this pursuit and was still not allowed in the offices, but he kept giving and giving.

Hopefully you have recognized that Bill needed to get to the decision maker, which in this case was the CFO. One of the things Bill asked for (QPQ for proceeding with the presentation) was that the CFO would be attending. Steve told Bill he would be attending all the presentations.

Bill and his team showed up for the presentation that they prepared for over twenty hours. They were determined to show why Southern Company should select Indus. They were out to prove the Wishbone disaster Southern Company had experienced should not be an issue, based on the new combined product.

Right before Bill started the presentation, he noticed the CFO was not in attendance. When he mentioned this to Steve, Steve apologized and explained the CFO was called out of town on other business.

You should always confirm the day before to ensure the decision maker will be attending your presentation/meeting. If he/she is called out of town or something comes up, you can reschedule. Once you are already onsite, it becomes more difficult to reschedule.

Bill's presentation went well, as far as he could tell; Steve said it was great. Again, three weeks went by with no communication with Steve. Bill also called the CFO many times with no response at all. A few days later, Bill got a letter in the mail requesting a pricing proposal. This was when Bill said we didn't understand.

Just because someone asks you to send a proposal or asks for pricing doesn't mean he/she is any more interested than he/she was before. For example, we have one very large client that everyone in our market space asks pricing from. Almost every time, that pricing is used to comparison shop smaller vendors. It took us some time to prove this to them and change how they were doing their proposals.

Bill needed a game changer. He had to get in front of the CFO. The advice was clear: Do not give them the pricing, share your feelings, and exchange the pricing for a meeting with the CFO to present it in person. If the CFO wouldn't meet with Bill, then there was no way Southern Company would spend $25 million with Indus. Bill was not comfortable with this approach at all, but to his credit he followed the plan. He let me know that when he delivered the message, Steve was not happy.

To make a long story longer, three days later Bill and the Indus team were invited to present their numbers to the CFO and present their case. Bill had tried for nine months to get this meeting. In the end, Indus did win most of the business, about $16 million of it. Everyone agreed that without the meeting with the CFO, which they only got due to holding out the pricing, they would have never won any of the Southern Company business.

Remember, with the QPQ Sales approach, you have to establish a give-and-take relationship. To do this, you sometimes have to say, "I will if you will." Sometimes you have to say, "No." It works, especially if you sound like a professional, prepare like a professional, and act like a professional. Professional defined as: knowing your business, knowing the prospects business, offering prudent solutions, and being a collaborative partner in the process.

CHAPTER 5

DEVELOPING MUTUAL RESPECT WITH QPQ

Do you feel you are getting the respect you want and desire from your prospects? The Transformational QPQ Sales approach is designed to help you stay in control of your sales pursuits and create collaboration between you and your prospects while establishing relationships based on mutual respect. When all three of these things are in alignment, you win business, and your job is a lot more satisfying.

Over the years, I learned not everyone is made up with the same sales DNA. It is easier for some and harder for others to break the old habits of being in a subservient position with clients and prospects. It is a real transformation in attitude and actions to break this pattern. The application of QPQ should never be arrogant or confrontational. If a sales situation becomes contentious between you and your prospect, more times than not, it is their issue, not yours. To apply QPQ and build a relationship based on mutual respect, the first thing has to be respect for yourself.

RESPECT YOURSELF

You can buy Bruce Willis's song "Respect Yourself" as a ringtone for your cell phone. "Respect yourself, respect yourself, if you don't respect yourself, ain't nobody gonna give a good ca-hoot, na na na, oh oh, respect yourself." You might not need or want that as your ringtone, but you should consider how you interact with your prospects in this regard. Think about whether you empower them to treat you in a way that is disrespectful. Use a standard of measurement you would apply to anyone. Don't discount it in some way because you are in selling situations. Of course, most people will say to themselves right off that they do respect themselves. I'm not sure about this after some of the interactions I have witnessed in sales situations.

EQUAL AND WORTHY

Why would you ever think you are anything other than equal to the people you are selling to? Because someone is older, makes more money, or has a bigger title or office, does that mean they are better than you in some way? We all have issues, concerns, and stresses in our lives. It is all part of being human. Of course, you are worthy to anyone you might be calling on. Aren't you sincerely trying to help the people you are selling to? You are calling on people to provide a service or a product that will enhance their business in some way. It's not unusual to get very anxious before you call on a senior executive, especially when you are younger. I got over that pretty quickly when I was sitting in a meeting with the founders of the company I worked for, a board member, and the rest of the executive team.

MAKING IT UP

All the executives were gathered around a large board-room table discussing the quarter's numbers, the current pipeline of opportunities, and what the year-end numbers would look like. My boss was out of town, and for some reason he thought I might get something out of attending this meeting. I sat sheepishly in the corner, listening and trying to learn something from these people who were obviously much smarter than I was. Just like most of these types of meetings, they talked about the products, the market, and our positioning. Don't ask me why, but at one point I felt compelled to offer a suggestion. As soon as I spoke up, the entire room went silent, and all eyes turned toward me. I just about wet my pants. I thought, "OMG, these guys are really listening to me."

Everything seemed to move in slow motion at this point, and all I wanted to do was not to look like a fool.

After the meeting, the founder of the company came up to me laughing and pointed out how startled I looked in the meeting when I spoke up. That didn't help me feel more equal, but what he said next has stuck with me my entire life. He said, *"You think because of our age, experience, and position we have this thing all figured out. We don't at all! We are making it up every day as we go along."* He went on to thank me for my input and let me know I had some good ideas. Understand that all CEOs and management teams search every day for the answers. Realizing this will help you stand tall and communicate with conviction as you approach them with solutions. Never feel anything other than equal to the people you are calling on.

THE BOARD

How many times has your proposal gone to the board for approval? Honestly, what is your first thought when you hear "the board" about anything? Most salespeople find "the board" intimidating. The perception is that the board is some secret society with special handshakes and rituals, and all the board members wear ceremonial robes and sacrifice some farm animal before every meeting. Be very wary of the board, because each member has a superpower they reveal only in this meeting.

Let me dispel the myths for you. Being a former board member for a publicly held company, I will tell you that a board meeting is a bunch of people sitting around the table talking about the business, trying to sort out the best path for the future, making sure shareholders' interests are being served well, and reviewing current results. It is no different from the meeting I described to you that I sat in with the founders when I was in my early twenties. Don't shy away from the board. You should apply QPQ to presenting in front of the board vs. letting someone do your selling for you.

MUTUAL RESPECT AT THE TOP

I would be remiss if we didn't review applying the Transformational QPQ Selling approach at the top. You could read this book, digest every word in it, and execute each aspect of what it offers you, but if you apply your newfound skills to the wrong person in the organization, you will often still fall short in your selling efforts.

As mentioned earlier, the world we live in has changed in recent years. Information and knowledge are being transferred at rates never seen before. Buyers are more educated and demand more from their suppliers and salespeople. In today's market, decision makers expect salespeople to know their offerings. More importantly, they demand that sellers understand their business as well. To become the coveted "trusted advisor," sellers must not only understand the executive's business, but they must also relate to them on a personal basis. If they are unable to do so, then they will be perceived as just another quota salesperson, with the only objective being to sell something.

Regardless of the industry, the market is tight. Organizations are under pressure for results. More importantly, decision makers are being held accountable for their decisions and the results they achieve. Salespeople face new competitors in the market regularly. Most reps consider status quo as the number-one foe. Status quo is the prospect doing nothing. They don't buy from a competitor, they just keep doing things the way they always have or keep using whatever they have always use. In the current market environment, the ability to sell business solutions rather than products or services is essential. This can only be done effectively at the executive level.

SELLING TO EXECUTIVES

Understanding the unique business and personal challenges of selling to executives is crucial to success. Executives today are people who have little time or patience for "quota carrying" salespeople. They are working longer hours, answering to more people, and have limited amount of time.

Salespeople need to establish credibility early in the sales cycle, both for themselves and for their company. How can they make the most of such limited time to establish trust and gain continued access to the executives?

TRUSTED ADVISOR STATUS

Many sales organizations today boast that they have a consultative sales approach. What this implies is that their salespeople form a consultant-type relationship with the decision makers in the organizations they are selling to. Executives buy because they feel understood. "Understood" is defined as the salespeople knowing their business and knowing their personal challenges inside of the business. People want salespeople to "get them." People don't buy because they understand. Salespeople typically spend a lot of time and effort trying to get prospects to understand the benefits of their products and services. Understanding this statement is the key for moving forward and establishing yourself as a trusted advisor to your prospects and clients. When someone represents himself/herself as having a consultative sales approach, I ask the following questions.

EXECUTIVE APPITUDE TEST

If you can answer all the questions below, then you are way ahead of most. Most salespeople say they could answer some of the questions on the test, but not in much detail. It's hard to be a trusted advisor or have a consultative sales approach if you don't fully understand the executive you are calling on.

- **How are the executives you call on evaluated?**
- **What keeps them awake at night?**
- **What are their hot buttons?**
- **What are the top ten issues this executive has?**
- **Why do they have these issues?**

If you truly understand this, it might significantly change

- **Who else in the organization is affected by these issues?**
- **What gets someone in this executive fired or promoted?**
- **Can you discuss industry trends with this executive?**
- **Can you relate your solution is each issue in detail?**

your sales approach. We are all classically trained to present, show, tell, and explain in painstaking detail what we have to offer. Today, you have to show up with what I refer to as "prospect knowledge."

PROSPECT KNOWLEDGE

There are two forms of prospect knowledge: personal and professional. Professional prospect knowledge is what most salespeople are used to and understand: industry terms, industry trends, corporate challenges, marketplace issues, and business problems.

Personal prospect knowledge is different and is more important to know. This also has a couple of levels:

A. How the issues and challenges affect your prospect personally in their career and job.

B. How the issues and challenges affect them personally at home.

As an example, you might understand how being three versions behind on software updates affects the CIO. Sellers then must communicate their understanding of potential disasters. When you communicate how that situation might affect the CIO, then it becomes easier to collaborate with them to sort out a solution because he/she is three versions behind, the maintenance has been voided. If the system goes down, there is no way to fix it. He/she could lose his/her job if this happens. Because this situation exists, the CIO has to work weekends to sort this out. Because he/she is working on weekends, he/she is missing his/her son's Little League games, which is causing issues at home. Most issues at work spill over to our personal lives and affect us. Everyone would appreciate help or solutions for anything that is affecting him/her at home.

FINDING PROSPECT KNOWLEDGE

The question is often asked, "How do I find this information?" From a professional standpoint, you can gain prospect knowledge by reading the same periodicals that decision makers read. Magazines like *CFO*, *CIO*, all contain information that will help you transform into a trusted advisor. You probably have established clients in these roles. They would be happy to sit with you for an hour over lunch and explain every aspect of their role. People tend to like to talk about themselves, especially if someone is sincerely interested. You might even have whatever role you want to learn about in the company you work for. Have you ever sat down with your CFO, CIO, or CEO and asked them to answer all the questions on the executive aptitude test for you? They will not only help you, they will be impressed you have asked them for their help.

Gaining personal prospect knowledge is even easier. To do this, it is as simple as asking your prospect how this project, this issue, and so on will or might affect him/her personally. Selling is about relationships, right? The core of a relationship is the personal aspect. Many sellers have very long-term relationships with their clients, but even then they are reluctant to ask personal, probing questions. This isn't a game or some clever sales tactic. You should only ask this question if you care and you want to make a difference. If a prospect sees you are sincere, and you are sincere about helping them, then the relationship and the interactions will develop.

Besides the above suggestions for gaining prospect knowledge, consider this simple step-by-step approach.

Step 1

Determine who is typically the final decision maker. This should be easy.

- Ask your manager.
- Review past agreements to see who signed them.
- Ask other successful salespeople.
- Ask the prospect.

Step 2

Find out information on how to relate to executives.

- Search the company website for personal data.
- Read the annual report.

-   Read recent news releases and look for quotes.
-   Be a friend to the "gatekeeper" and ask him/her questions.

Step 3

Become a trusted advisor. How? You might not have ever been a CFO, CEO, or VP, but you have to put yourself in his/her shoes and relate to him/her at his/her level. There are several ways to gather this knowledge that will give you the ability to create relationships based on mutual respect at the top.

-   Interview executives in your own company who hold the role you need information about.
-   Ask your friends who might have this role.
-   Network with people who might know someone in this role. Ask them to introduce you, and then interview them.

PROSPECT KNOWLEDGE TRAINING

I believe understanding your prospects at this level is one of the most important things you can do. You will find them to be collaborative, more respectful, and open to you. What happens in most organizations when they hire a new salesperson is they spend a few days or weeks in some internal company orientation. Most of the time this orientation is spent on all the features and functions of the products or services the company provides. You might even spend some time on the competitive differences you will enjoy while you are out in the marketplace selling. Think back, how much time is ever spent talking about the people you should be selling to? It's a requirement that sellers gain knowledge about the role of each person they approach in the sales cycle. By truly relating to them on their level, a completely different level of respect will unfold. Those outstanding bells and whistles of unsurpassed service you are about to offer now will be much better received.

TODAY'S MARKETS

In many surveys taken from both executives and sales-people in recent years, most sellers are not perceived as business consultants. There are various reasons for this. The overwhelming reason is that most sellers do not take the actions laid out in this book. Instead, they recite the company's marketing literature in hopes it will resonate with the buyer.

Salespeople have been taught over the years to sell the features and benefits of their products. As the years evolved, this was extended to selling features, benefits, and solutions. The best salespeople took this one step further. They sold features, benefits, and solutions and differentiated their solutions from other alternatives, including the status quo, that were available to decision makers. In the current marketplace, sellers have to do better and evolve once again.

NO DECISION

There are various reports that show 40 percent of sales-people face such bouts of call reluctance at some point in their careers that it costs them their jobs. If we added one word in front of call reluctance—executive, or executive call reluctance—this percentage would double.

In my experience, 98 percent of salespeople sell at the wrong level, especially early in the sales cycle. The application of QPQ is designed to help you get higher in the account faster. Salespeople typically spend their time with Dilbert—"influencers" or "recommenders" vs. decision makers.

BUYING A HOUSE IN DILBERTVILLE

You recall earlier we defined who Dilbert is. Again, Dilbert is the person who acts with authority, but is not the decision maker. The project leader at 3M would be considered Dilbert, as an example. All Dilberts and Dilbertas live in Dilbertville. Dilbertville is a comfortable area where many sellers like to live. This is the area of the organization that has only influencers, recommenders, and people who do not make decisions. Sellers seem to relate to the people in Dilbertville and develop good relationships with them. In Dilbertville sellers feel they get a good level of respect. All the houses are in the same price range, and people are just pretty darn friendly. Sounds good, so what is the issue with laying down roots in Dilbertville? The answer is everything. It's OK to visit your friends in Dilbertville and drive through there once in a while, but you want to buy a house on Park Avenue, where all the decision makers live who can make an impact on your success. No one ever really moves up from Dilbertville. Sellers can easily get stuck at the wrong level just selling to influencers and recommenders. It's like the small town everyone wants to grow up in and move away from, but never does. You can't grow and prosper in Dilbertville. The 3M project leader wanted me just to stay with him, and he did everything he could to prevent me from meeting with the decision maker and moving uptown. Think about some of your current pursuits that are stuck in Dilbertville. I will bet your business is not thriving there. Let's compare your shop in Dilbertville to the store you have set up on Park Avenue. Here's the nice thing: It doesn't cost you any more to set up shop on Park Avenue than it does in Dilbertville. In other words, if you work with decision makers, you will find your sales pursuits to be much more productive, shorter, and more profitable.

THE VILLAGE OF DILBERTVILLE

When I first started my career in software sales, my manager was going to show me how to sell. Our product was enterprise resource planning (ERP) software, which we hoped to sell to Xerox. This type of software usually comes with a six-figure licensing fee and has a long sales cycle. My manager was a West Point graduate. He was quite disciplined and followed exact procedures. I have to admit, he was pretty sure of himself, too. He let me know his every thought and move throughout this entire sales cycle. The "decision maker" (who was really Dilbert in disguise) on this account loved him. He would always gladly give him time, talk for hours about anything, and enjoy his company. It was coming to the end of the quarter, and of course, Xerox was on my manager's list as a definite closing prospect.

Unfortunately, my mentor on this account forgot to sell to the other people making the recommendations to the decision maker, and he did not qualify his prospect, now a friend, thoroughly enough. He didn't get outside of Dilbertville, and thus did not identify the true decision maker. The result was that Xerox bought from the competition.

What happened was my sales manager started believing everything he was hearing from Dilbert during this sales cycle. It's absolutely critical to qualify early, often, and all through the selling cycle. Not doing so is similar to an athlete reading and believing his or her own press, a fatal mistake. In regard to Xerox, a note came in the mail to my manager. The note went on and on about how great a salesperson my manager was, how professional he was, and how much the prospect liked him. The part I liked was the line that said, "You were the best sales rep I have ever had call on me." Since I was learning, I thought it was all right to ask, "How much do you get paid for second place in a software evaluation?" You can guess the rest.

If my manager were the best rep ever, he would have identified the decision maker, leveraged his relationship with Dilbert by applying QPQ, and won the business. If he were the best rep ever, I wonder who the other rep was, the one who got the business. In sales, you don't get anything for coming in second.

PERCEPTION IS REALITY

When you're selling, how you, your company, and your company's solution are perceived means everything. In my experience, the perception is generally far more important than the reality in any situation.

Most good dads are perceived as some kind of a hero by their kids. Maybe some fathers are heroes in some way. However, most of us are just regular guys, doing the best we can. Virtually all successful salespeople realize that understanding how people perceive them is one of the keys to sales success. If your kids think you are a hero, whether you are or aren't, isn't important. If they think you are a hero, then you are, at least to them, and that is the reality of the situation. That perception is reality is especially true in sales. If you act and come across like every other quoted salesperson, then that is what you will be to your prospects.

SALES SECURITY SYSTEM

You need to always be aware of each prospect's "sales security system." Every one of us has this system. It gets turned on like a force field when we think a sales rep is trying to sell us something. When the sales security system is turned on, it's practically impossible to sell any-one anything or be seen as a trusted advisor.

Since being perceived as a salesperson activates this force field, let's consider what triggers the alarm. Here are some reasons why you might be perceived as a salesper-son. Prospects think that:

1. Sellers are totally subservient to them.
2. Sellers are on commission, all they care about is mak-ing a sale.
3. You don't *really* care about their needs and issues.
4. Feel you don't listen.
5. You're trying to take advantage of them.
6. You do not have any personal knowledge of them.

Although there are additional triggers, those noted above are very common. Now let's consider how, if you want to be successful in sales, you should be perceived.

HOW YOU SHOULD BE PERCEIVED

Being a sales representative is a worthy profession. Unfortunately, salespeople often are embarrassed to tell others what they do for a living. How many times have you heard salespeople make up some fancy title for themselves when asked about their profession? The usual answer is that they are district managers or regional area managers. However, when you dig a little further, they are sales reps.

The reason so many reps try to make themselves out to be something other than salespeople is that negative connotations are often attached to the profession. Some common perceptions about salespeople is that they are the following:

1. Dishonest
2. Greedy
3. Indifferent
4. Self-centered—you're not listening
5. Sneaky

These are misperceptions. Most salespeople are honest and hardworking. However, as with any profession, the highly publicized bad actions of a minority of salespeople have given the rest of us a very bad name. Not only that, these misperceptions are ingrained throughout our society. People everywhere expect the worst from salespersons. That's why our sales security systems come on.

To succeed in sales, you need to be perceived as a trusted advisor.

It should be rewarding to you that you've helped someone solve a problem. If your interest is genuine, respect, job satisfaction, and results will follow.

Another thing to remember is that you don't want to be perceived as a threat to anyone while you're selling. Certainly, when I'm consulting, no one's afraid of me. No one needs to turn on the sales security system. A good consultant comes across as having a sincere objective of helping. As I stated, the best consultants actually have a genuine interest in helping.

"Your time is limited, so don't waste it living someone else's life. Don't be trapped by dogma, which is living with the results of other people's thinking. Don't let the noise of others' opinions drown out your own inner voice. And, most importantly, have the courage to follow your heart and intuition."

—Steve Jobs

CHAPTER 6

THE VALUE OF NO

You are a salesperson; they are the prospects, so it is your responsibility to provide them with whatever, whenever they want it. If you don't, then you will have no chance to sell them anything. You will alienate them, and they will buy from your competitor. This is the typical thought process of most sales professionals. Whoever bends over backward, and the furthest, wins the business. Right? This is absolutely wrong. There is a service aspect to selling that is important to understand. You are in the selling-solutions-to-business profession; you're not in the service business. Waiters, flight attendants, and bartenders are in the business of providing a service; you are in the business of selling. It is important that you understand where the line is.

THE POKER PARALLEL

To apply the Transformational QPQ sales approach effectively, you have to be willing to simply say no to your prospect at some point in the sales cycle. That will be nerve racking and likely cause some anxious moments. Just like in a Texas hold 'em poker game; to win you have to go all in and risk all your chips at some point. For those of you who don't play tournament hold 'em, everyone starts on equal ground with the same number of chips. The winner is the one person in the end who has every chip. Each player decides what hands they will play, how many chips to bet, and what hands to fold or say no to playing. If you put too many chips in the pot with a bad hand, you will likely lose.

You're not a poker player; you're a sales professional. If we revisit the number of sales pursuits each year that end up with a no decision, status quo, or that are lost to a competitor, I think you will understand the poker parallel. Too many times sellers spend a lot of time on opportunities that don't buy. There are countless reasons for this. Maybe your service or product is not a great fit (weak cards), or perhaps the prospect was just kicking tires and not serious. There's always a chance someone else has a better solution (better cards), and there's always that remote chance you got outsold (outplayed). In the game of poker, the winner isn't always the one with the best cards all the time. Over the course of a long two- or three-day tournament, the chip leader is the person who outplays the other players. This is true over the course of a sales cycle, too. As just one example of this, the person who is first to become a trusted advisor to the decision maker will typically carry the day, even if someone else has a better product and maybe even a better price.

WHEN YOU SHOULD FOLD

Folding your hand in poker is saying, "No, I am not going to play this hand, or I'm not going to invest that much on this hand." Most sellers I interact with do not have a big enough pipeline of opportunities, so any opportunity looks good to pursue. The mindset often is, "If I am not in the game, I have no chance to win." Yes, that is true, but you want your best chance to win because you have a limited amount of time and resources to invest. If you sit patiently in a poker tournament for a long period of time without good cards coming your way, pretty soon any two cards look good. The difference in sales is you don't have to wait for good opportunities to come your way; you can go out and find them.

We would all be the best poker players in the world if we didn't like the cards we were being dealt, so we folded them, but then picked up the deck and selected the cards we liked. Wait a minute, as a sales professional, you get to do that! Be selective and prospect to find the opportunities you can win! There are many alarms you should fold an opportunity and find ones you can win. Some of these are the following:

FOLD

There are only ten reasons to fold on this list. Of course, there could be many more. If you just stick to these ten and apply them to your current pipeline of prospects, I will bet you should fold 30 percent of them.

- When your access is blocked from the decision maker.
- The decision maker is nonresponsive.
- A Quid Pro Quo relationship cannot be established.
- If relationships aren't based on mutual respect.
- Your solution is not a good fit.
- There is a bias for another solution.
- There is no sponsor or champion in the account for you.
- When commitments are constantly broken and not followed through by the prospect.
- When the playing ground is not level.
- The prospect is unreasonable in their expectations.

THE SALES STRATEGY OF NO

The sales strategy of no seems like an oxymoron. One question we ask every group in our QPQ course is, *"How many times in your sales career have you told a prospect no, and had a negative result?"*

After thinking hard for a few seconds, no one can think of a single situation where saying no hurt them. Of course, there are situations where someone said no to a price, and the prospect didn't buy. In that situation, if the sales rep used no early enough in the sales cycle, he/she had a positive result. This is positive because the rep didn't waste time pursuing an opportunity that couldn't afford or wouldn't pay what the solution cost. In almost every circumstance when no was used, either the dynamics of the sales cycle changed a bit, or as a seller, you saved a lot time and effort with someone who wasn't going to buy anyway. Don't be afraid to use no as part of your sales strategy, especially with a difficult prospect.

QUALIFIED YES

Even though no one on the planet likes to hear no to anything, you still have to use it from time to time. Before you draw a line in the sand and say no, try offering a qualified yes. A qualified yes is simply offering options. If you have or had young children, you are probably already a pro at applying qualified yes's. As parents, we all hate saying no to our darling angels. They sometimes throw a fit, cry, and make the most pitiful, sad faces that pull on our heartstrings. As parents, we learn the art of negotiating with our kids pretty early in their lives.

Tyler wants to go see the latest Disney movie. He is counting on it, and in some way feels he is entitled to see this movie. You have to take him right now. You can say no and then be victim to the five-year-old's meltdown, or offer Tyler some options. "Tyler, we can't go see the movie, but instead we can do a puzzle together, read a book, or maybe I can find a fun movie on TV." Tyler still wants to go see the Disney movie, but now he has reasonable options to think about and consider.

You might be thinking that is good parenting advice for dealing with children, but what about my prospects? Really? Don't prospects often want what they want, and expect you to deliver it, regardless if it is reasonable or not? That program will soon be over as you learn the art of applying QPQ. If possible, we always want to offer reasonable options. If they are still demanding and will not accept one of the options, then you have to use no. If that doesn't work, then we execute the strategic withdrawal we discussed in Chapter 3.

CASE STUDY OF NO

This is a story about a sales cycle that makes this point and demonstrates many of the principles of applying no and, in the end, a qualified yes to a demanding prospect. We were selling to Southwest Portland Cement Company in Houston, Texas. One of the sales reps asked me to accompany him on a trip to Texas for a short presentation. There was a question-and-answer session with thirty of their controllers scheduled. The sales rep had done a good job with qualification from a solutions standpoint, and we felt this was a great fit for us. At the time, I was a senior executive for a small, but growing, self-funded company.

When we showed up, the room was filled with accountants, controllers, and the decision maker. We had done our homework, talked to noncompetitive sales people who had worked on this account and were informed, Larry, who was the CIO had a huge ego. I had made prior arrangements to leave early to attend a meeting at the home office in Hyannis, Massachusetts.

Before I left, Larry wanted me to see his computer room. I cannot say which is more exciting, seeing a computer room full of hardware or watching paint dry. We weren't selling hardware, so why did I need to see the computer room? We went to see his computer room. He went on and on about the different pieces of computer hardware, the configurations, and the special flooring he had installed. At the same time, he let me know exactly what he expected from us if we were going to do business together. He let me know that Southwest Portland Cement was an IBM showcase account. This meant a lot of people would be coming to visit them to see the latest technologies available and to see what they were using, and who they were working with. This could mean a lot of business to our company. That was the first thing that set off the alarms in my head. If you recall, I had heard that exact same speech from Georgia Pacific the year before. Because the company was an IBM showcase account, he expected a 50 percent discount, a fulltime person onsite helping them implement the solution, and several other things. I listened intently, knowing the entire time we were not going to accommodate one thing on his long list. Every time I tried to bring up those things we would not do to accommodate him, he just talked over me and reminded me about being an IBM showcase account.

When I got to the home office, I called the sales rep and told him about my conversation. I told him not to waste his time on this account, because even if we could meet the decision maker's unreasonable expectations, there was no way he would pay our price or accept our contract terms. This was a direct example of telling the prospect no, thank you.

A few days later I received a call from Larry. It was Thursday afternoon when he called to let me know he wanted to meet our consulting team in Houston on Tuesday morning. I informed him that we did not pull people off projects to travel to prospects, and we would not be coming to Houston. He was very indignant when he heard this, and was quick to let me know our competition was very happy to accommodate him. Again, I apologized, withdrew from the opportunity, and declined his request to go back to Texas.

A few days later he called again and wanted to know if he could bring his team to Hyannis to take a deeper look at our process, people, and company. If he were willing to fly six people across the country to see us, then I was willing to give them an hour of my time.

THE VALUE OF NO

It was kind of funny when the Southwest Portland Cement team arrived, because they had just come from the competitor's home office. I guess they would not go to Houston either. Keep in mind, prospects will not always tell you the truth. They will apply pressure on you by throwing alternative solutions in your face. The founder of the company I worked for wasn't usually involved in sales meetings with prospects. There was a good reason why the founder of this company wasn't involved. He was the leading member of the sales-prevention team, so we tried to keep prospects away from him. For some reason, he chose on this day to sit in on the meeting. I didn't even have a chance to prep him on the conversation in Houston before we started the meeting.

Larry sat at the head of the big conference table, and our founder sat at the other end. To start the meeting, Larry sat back and said, "Bob, I apologize for not talking to you about this first, but Mr. President, we almost didn't come up here today. Getting anything out of your sales force has been like pulling teeth. We don't think you want our business, and we don't appreciate the treatment we have received through our evaluation of your solutions." You can only imagine the look I received from the founder of the company. Truly, if looks could kill, I'd be dead right now. Stop and think, what would you have done at this point?

I quickly jumped in and asked the president if he wanted me to address Larry's comments. With smoke coming out of the president's ears, he replied, "I wish you would." With that, I said, "Larry, what you told me in Houston was that you are an IBM showcase account and wanted a 50 percent discount, a person to stay onsite until you are fully implemented, and…is that correct?" I asked. He leaned back in his chair with a kind of smirk on his face, and he said, "Absolutely." At that point, I stood up, put my hand out, and said, "Let's end this meeting now so you guys can enjoy a nice day on the Cape." As if we had rehearsed it, the founder stood up also and extended his hand as well and said, "It was sure nice to meet all of you." I couldn't believe the founder stood up on cue and did that. It was perfect. It was like hitting the sweet spot on your driver and seeing the ball fly three hundred yards right down the middle of the fairway. That happens about once in a lifetime and this founder doing the right thing in a sales situation was about the same. If you haven't recognized it yet, that was the no.

Larry looked confused, and flustered. I reminded him again of his wish list and expectations. Then I let him know that was not a prudent way to evaluate. We could not meet any of his expectations, so why waste any more time? As firmly and as directly as possible, I said, "Now, if you were going to evaluate based on the strength of the company, the people, our expertise, and how we can meet your business requirements, I know we would win your business. That is not what you are telling us your evaluation criteria are, so…" That was the qualified yes.

He quickly recanted, sat down, and said those were the important things and that his lists were just nice things to have. I really got a lot of satisfaction out of that. I again, very clearly, reset the expectations. I made sure Larry and his team were crystal clear that we were not going to do *anything* he came into that meeting demanding. They all understood, and we continued the next day.

The end of this story was that Southwest Portland Cement selected us and paid list price for our services, and we did not accommodate one item on their list. What is really ironic, is that Larry ended up being one of our best references.

This story sets the stage for many principles for QPQ Selling and using no or the qualified yes in a sales pursuit. If you reread the story, it will become clear what the underlying foundation is. The give-and-take part of this sales cycle, combined with some direct bold stances, is what made the difference. Controlling the prospect and being perceived as a business consultant vs. a canned, slick salesperson is professional selling.

Before they read this book, I think many sales reps would have handled the Southwest Portland Cement situation much differently. At best, they would have had a longer sales cycles. They likely would have had to discount their price for the privilege of being installed in an IBM showcase account. Worst case, they would have not won the business. Once it was made crystal clear SWPC was not going to dictate to us all the terms of the sales cycle, and they were going to have a give-and-take relationship or we would walk away from the opportunity, the dynamics changed 100 percent. In this situation, we gave away almost nothing. As you go through each chapter, each concept and principle, think through some of the opportunities you have had. Think about how you could have applied QPQ to them and the difference it could have made. Would your results have been different?

A fundamental concept in selling is understanding you will not be successful by only trying to give prospects what you believe they want. To be successful, you have to provide prospects with what they need.

JIM CARREY SALES APPROACH

Hopefully you are familiar with the actor Jim Carrey. He has had leading roles in major productions such as *Dumb and Dumber*, *The Mask*, *Liar Liar*, *The Truman Show*, *Man on the Moon*, and many more.

One of my favorites is the movie *Dumb and Dumber*. It was in this movie I recognized what I call the Jim Carrey sales approach, which many sellers unknowingly apply. In this movie, Carrey's character, Lloyd, is the biggest moron who could have possibly walked the earth. He was a social misfit. His fantasy love obsession is played by Lauren Holly, whose character's name is Mary and is a stunning beauty who exudes grace and elegance and has a charming personality. Mary and Lloyd are standing in the living room, and Lloyd awkwardly asks Mary what the chances would be that they could… Mary without hesitation replies, "The chances of that happening are one in a million!" Without hesitation Lloyd (Carrey) excitingly shouts out, *"So you say there's a chance!"*

We get involved in thousands of QPQ deal reviews every year. I am sad to say, too many times the Jim Carrey sales approach is applied—that being defined as, "There is a chance." It's a remote chance, a one-in-a-million chance, of actually seeing any revenue from the pursuit. Just like Lloyd, who never realized his fantasy with Mary, even though he went to the ends of the Earth pursuing her, sellers applying the Jim Carrey sales approach rarely, if ever, close the sale.

THE BLIND SQUIRREL

It is not unusual for us to have a spirited discussion in our workshops about whether salespeople should or shouldn't fill out a blind request for proposal (RFP). It is a rare occurrence that a seller receives an RFP that they knew nothing about, fills it out, and ends up winning the business. I tell every group that the worst thing that could happen in their career is that one time in 2002 you filled out a blind RFP and won the business. You will always want to go after this type of unqualified and costly opportunity if you won a blind RFP one time. The saying goes, "A blind squirrel finds a nut every once in a while." So what? The acid test on this issue is that if it cost you personally $10,000 to fill out and respond to the RFP, would you spend your own money to do this? If you won that one time in 2002 and your pipeline is less than robust, you might say yes. But you will be broke in no time if your answer was yes. Applying the Jim Carrey sales approach of "there's a chance" is not a good strategy and will end up in disappointment, costing you lots of money and waste time.

IN vs. INTO

"In" means you show up physically. You're in a room. "Into" means that you're totally absorbed—physically, mentally, and emotionally.

The following quote describes the "into" quality best. It is from Rob Gilbert, editor, *Bits & Pieces*.

Painters paint with their hands.

Artists paint with their hands and minds.

But masters paint with their hands and minds through their hearts.

Just because:

- You go to class does not mean you are a student.
- You can sing a song does not mean that you're a singer.
- You sell something does not necessarily mean that you're a salesperson.
- You're *in* a profession does not mean that you're a professional.

Gilbert goes on to say, "Successful students, singers, salespeople, and other professionals have developed the skill of being absorbed physically, mentally, and emotionally. Being *in* something does not mean you'll get anything *out* of it. The only way you'll ever totally get the most *out of* it, is if you are totally *into* it."

You can choose to keep on conducting business exactly the same way you have always done it. You can sell the same way, approach prospects the same way, and think the same way, without making any changes. If you aren't applying QPQ, not offering qualified yeses or saying no, then you will likely not get a transformation in your results.

THE BOTTOM LINE

The concepts and principles in this book are different from what you might have read or applied before. Not everyone will adopt all the principles in this book. Not everyone who earns a living in sales is successful either. Richard L. Weaver II summed it up in a speech he cited in *Executives Speeches*:

> Face it, nobody owes you a living. What you achieve or fail to achieve in your lifetime is directly related to what you do, or fail to do. People don't choose their parents or childhood, but you can choose your own direction. Everyone has problems and obstacles to overcome, but that too is relative to each individual. Nothing is carved in stone; you can change anything in your life if you want to badly enough.

Excuses are for losers. Those who take responsibility for their actions are the real winners in life.

Winners meet life's challenges head on, knowing there are no guarantees, and give all they've got. And never think it's too early to begin. Time plays no favorites and will pass whether you act or not. Take control of your life. Dare to dream and take risks… Compete."

Everyone who is reading this can make a transformation and change the outcome of their results.

CHAPTER 7

CREATIVITY

Before every QPQ course, we ask participants what they would like to get out of the next couple of days. Without exception, the most common request people have is to differentiate themselves from the others in the market.

TRANSFORMATION BY DIFFERENTIATION

Several years ago I was standing in front of a class of about thirty people. This was a group of salespeople who sold commercial printing. I asked the above question and got the differentiation answer as usual. This time it was a little different, though. The group asked me how much knowledge I had about commercial printing.

From all angles of the room, I heard questions like, "Do you know what four-color printing entails?" "Do you know about all the different paper choices?" "Can you describe the different types of printing presses?" "Do you know what aqueous paper is and how it is used?" The answers were no, no, no, and no. Then someone shouted out from the back of the room, "How can you possibly help us differentiate ourselves from all the other commercial printers if you don't know any of this?" For the first time, I was facing a class mutiny.

I'll admit I was a little flustered by the expectation that I was supposed to be a commercial-printing expert. After the group members finished expressing their concerns, what I told them was true for them and everyone else:

Regardless of what you are selling, the best way to differentiate from all the other alternatives is to be yourself as an individual.

Always keep in mind that your company (in this case Offset Atlanta Printing) never sold anything to XYZ Company. Sales are always made by two individuals working together. As an individual, how you interact, the relationships you establish, and sometimes the creativity you display are what will differentiate you from the pack. Unique solutions come and go.

Of course, it is terrific if you work for an organization that has a solution no one else in the marketplace has. When that situation occurs, selling is like shooting fish in a barrel. This unique situation is always short lived though. Someone is always working on building the next better mousetrap.

You should always work on building a better you. Changing the way you sell and applying all aspects of QPQ is different and new. This alone will differentiate you from other sellers who have subservient relationships with prospects, live in Dilbertville, and have no control of the sales cycle. Sometimes you will still have to step farther outside of the self-imposed box you have put yourself into. You have to differentiate yourself even further and apply some creativity in your sales pursuit.

CREATIVE TRANSFORMATION

Creativity is reaching beyond conventional limits or traditional wisdom in the pursuit of something new and different. The creative process is a powerful process we all need to invoke, regardless of our profession or pursuits. Everyone has some level of creativity inside of them.

The attentive, daily practice of creativity helps us to focus and break out of our comfort zone in these times when uncertainty seems to be assaulting us from every direction. Practicing creativity creates a fresh perspective and helps sellers reach their full potential. Do you remember when you were a kid, all the teacher needed to give you was a crayon and a blank piece of paper? Suddenly our creativity would come alive. We would create the most magical pictures anyone had ever seen; at least we thought so.

As we age, much of the time, that childhood creativity seems to disappear just when we need it the most. You must give birth to your ideas and creativity. They are your future waiting to be born. Respect your need to create.

Where is it said that you can't or shouldn't be creative in your selling efforts? Somewhere there must be a book that I have never found that defines the rules of engagement when selling. If everyone reads or subscribes to the same way to do things in a selling situation, then it is going to be impossible to ever differentiate yourself. This being the case, we should all be concerned that robots will soon put us all out of a job, because they can be programmed to follow the profession selling script.

Do the work necessary to strengthen your belief in your creative abilities and understand the importance of your creative acts. When we talk about being creative, we're not speaking about writing a poem or painting a picture, even though there's nothing wrong with those activities. We are speaking about *breaking the chains of the ordinary*.

My mom used to ask, as only mothers can, "If Billy ran his bike into a wall, would you too?" Of course, the answer was always no, and I felt like an idiot. From my observations consulting with many organizations around the world, I'm not sure the answer would always be no. It is astonishing to observe an entire group of people following the same actions as someone else when it is not getting the desired results. It's like watching a bunch of cows one by one following the cow in front of them to the slaughterhouse. You have to elevate your expectations for results and transform, or you won't get out of the box. Dare to be different, and follow your own vision.

I think most successful businesspeople would agree that if someone has a creative new idea that has been well thought out and well executed, but fails, that is acceptable. The alternative, which is never acceptable, is when there is no creativity, and the results are not achieved. It is far worse to just sit around, waiting for someone else to tell you what to do, than it is to think outside the box, trying to make something positive happen.

THE SELF-IMPOSED BOX

If we all followed the same paths, had the same processes, went through the same routines, never ventured out, and couldn't think for ourselves, we would be machines. It is the creative people who make a difference in the world we live in. There's not one person's name you would recognize as being successful who didn't perform a creative act at some point on their way to fame and fortune.

I often ask the people in our QPQ classes if anyone can relate a negative result when they did something creative in a sales pursuit. The disclaimer to the question is, "Provided it wasn't obnoxious." Most of the time the class just sits there staring at me and says nothing. So the follow-up question is, "Have any of you ever done anything creative in a sales pursuit before?" Every once in a while, someone will come up with something, but rarely has there been a story of a negative impact on the results when creativity was applied. So why don't sellers apply more creativity to their sales pursuits? The answer is that we stay in the box, which is a safe place where everyone knows what acceptable, professional business behavior is. I promise you that no one will ever thrive in the box.

NEW SHOES

How about you? When was the last time you got out of the box and did something creative? What is the most creative thing you have ever done? Both of these questions are standard interviewing questions for me. I want to measure how the interviewee thinks. The objective is to investigate their entrepreneurial spirit to determine if they are willing to try new things. Every organization needs individuals who have different visions and creativity, along with the courage to act on his/her ideas. It is vital to see if candidates can bring something unique to the table or are just going to follow the crowd.

Thousands of interviews later, one captivating story stands out in my mind. The fact that it stands out alone among all others is due to this person's creative out-of-the-box thinking. I was conducting one of my standard interviews and exploring this person's creativity, and I asked, "When was the last time you got out of the box and did something creative? What is the most creative thing you have ever done in business?" The candidate, Scott Johnson, told such a creative story I had to stop him twice. I wanted to know if he was putting me on, or if he actually did this.

Scott told me the most creative thing he did was sell his small company to Oracle. Scott said he had developed a unique product and knew it would be a perfect fit to augment Oracle's already robust solutions. As with any large company, there were a lot of levels of management and bureaucracy when you sell anything to them. Scott told me he had a few meetings and quickly determined the only way he was going to sell his company to Oracle was if he secured a meeting with Larry Ellison (CEO of Oracle). Getting a meeting with Mr. Ellison was not easy. He is not the type of person who sits in his office just waiting for the phone to ring, hoping someone will sell him something. It was going to take two ingredients if Scott was going to get to Oracle's CEO: persistence and creativity.

At this point, I was on the edge of my chair. I asked what happened next. He said he called Mr. Ellison's office every day, multiple times a day, for ten days. He would always get his administrative assistant, "the gatekeeper," and she would always tell him that Mr. Ellison was not available. With all the phone calls, Scott had developed a rapport with the gatekeeper.

Scott was committed to get this meeting, and his creativity kicked in. He solicited help from the gatekeeper to get this meeting with Mr. Ellison. He shared his plan with her, which was to buy a new pair of wingtip shoes. He would only put one shoe in the box. He would put a note in the shoe that said, "Now that I have one shoe in the door, I'll have the other at your office at 7:00 a.m. Wednesday." With that, he placed the note in the shoe and sent it off to Mr. Ellison's administrative assistant to place on his desk. She thought Scott's plan was extremely creative and was all for helping him. So Scott showed up at 7:00 a.m. Wednesday to have his meeting. Do you think Mr. Ellison was there waiting for him, and Scott had his meeting at 7:00 a.m.? If you guessed no, you were right. Scott sat there, and he finally got in at 10:00 a.m. Mr. Ellison said he had only five minutes. I guess that is all he needed, because Scott sold his company to Oracle two weeks later.

Creativity is almost always rewarded and appreciated. Scott had nothing to lose. There was no chance of selling the company without this meeting. He couldn't even get a returned phone call, so at this point Scott had two choices: walk away defeated, or get creative and try something different. He made the right choice.

One of the conscious choices you might have to make to effect change is set your priorities differently.

CREATIVITY

There is no perfect time to be creative. There is only now. Examine the myriad things you do in your daily life and eliminate time wasters and tasks that aren't necessary. The world won't end if you don't clean the dishes this exact minute, if you don't wash the car, or if you don't cut the grass in your yard even if it is an inch taller than your neighbor's. Put creativity high on your to-do list in large letters. When you are overwhelmed, it is hard to be creative. Your mind is racing off a thousand different places, thinking of the chores and tasks you have that lie in front of you. Just like the time you spend exercising, with your family, or watching TV, carve out some time to be and think creatively. There are always excuses, reasons, and justifications why we can't achieve, make it, and be creative. Those excuses are the sounds of complacency.

Think about the task of writing a book as just one example. It is an extremely time-consuming process that requires creative thinking. My current work requirement is about twelve hours a day, usually six days a week. On top of that, there are four kids and a spouse to support, an exercise regimen I am committed to, house projects, and too many other responsibilities to list. A friend of mine simply said, find just one hour a day to write my book. Get up an hour earlier or go to bed an hour later, but just commit the time to write one hour a day. It took some effort, but I found that hour. I ended up finding more than that, and I bet you can too.

CREATIVITY TO GO

Establish the practice of "creativity to go." Sometimes you may need long blocks of time to work on your ideas, but you can accomplish other steps in short bursts. Research magazines in the doctor's waiting room, sketch out ideas for your next venture, or brainstorm with your friends at the gym to get your creative juices flowing. Contrary to popular opinion, creativity and real life aren't mutually exclusive. When we mindfully work to put the two in balance, each enhances the other. There are many opportunities to think creatively every day, and the opportunities are all around you. The next time you walk in a restaurant, think what you might change to make it better. Apply this same creative eye everywhere you go. Think about potential improvements and what you might do differently. When you are looking in magazines and see the ads, ask yourself if they are creative and clever enough. How would you change them? Even as you read this book, think of how you would have written it to make it more impactful.

Over the years, my wife and I have bought and sold a lot of real estate. We find it a rewarding and sometimes a lucrative experience. My wife and I like to look at houses in all parts of the world. If we are in a new place for more than three days, we normally look at houses. We enjoy going in and investigating all the rooms, the layout, and the furniture placement. Each time we go through a house, we have a lively conversation of how we would change this or change that, or "if they only would have done this…" It's a way for us to be creative and get ideas for building our own house. That activity satisfies a lot of things; I spend time with the love of my life, we get to be creative together, we might find a solid investment, and we gather ideas and images for our own house. That's creativity when we are on the go.

I can appreciate that looking at houses with your wife may not be your favorite pastime, but the point is that there are many areas and many ways you can fit exercising the creative part of your mind into your active and busy schedule.

CREATIVE SAILING

Many years ago, I was calling on Lakeland Regional Medical Center, selling in the healthcare space. As long as it was ethical and professional, I would do anything to win business.

It is important to point out I had already established myself as a trusted advisor to this decision maker. The issue was the competition had also established the trusted-advisor status, and our solutions were very comparable. A creative and differentiating event was required to win this business.

The decision maker of the hospital was a highly experienced gentleman, and he was extremely tough. He was one of those guys who say, "OK, I've got fifteen minutes. What do you have?" I'm sure you know the type. He'd been a VP of sales, president of a company, and COO, so he had seen it all. It took me two lunches and another separate sales call to get him to even show me a crack in the door. Lakeland Regional Hospital represented a $750,000 opportunity. Because the decision maker was definitely going to buy from my competitor or me, it was worth a few more calls to open him up on a personal level.

I had to think of a way to differentiate myself from my competitor, but nothing was coming to me at all. Finally, at our second lunch, the decision maker explained he had moved to Florida from the Northeast because his wife suffered from severe asthma. Even though the hospital was in Lakeland, they lived in Sarasota, almost two hours away, because they both loved sailing. That was all I needed to hear. My creative switch turned on automatically. I told him my wife and I were planning a long weekend in Sarasota and had a forty-one-foot sailboat rented for the day. I asked him, since we'd both be in Sarasota, if he and his wife would like to join us? He gladly accepted and said he was looking forward to it.

Now all I had to do was find a forty-one-foot sailboat and a captain, convince my wife to come to Sarasota, and get my manager to approve the expenses for this excursion. I'm not much of a sailor. I get seasick very easily, but you have to do whatever it takes. I knew if I could get the decision maker and his wife out on the boat for the afternoon, my chances of winning his business would increase dramatically. I was pretty sure my competitor would not be renting a sailboat and taking him and his wife sailing too. This would be a differentiating event and would give me the inside track to prove we had the best solutions for the hospital.

I found a boat to rent and got the OK from my manager (as long as he could join us). I did have to make a deal with my wife to get her to come along. If I signed up this account, then she could buy all-new dining room furniture. So we were all set. The decision maker and his wife showed as scheduled, and we had a three-hour tour. Luckily, the result was not the same as it was for the SS *Minnow* and we weren't stranded on Gilligan's Island. Everyone got along great, and lots of personal information was exchanged.

When we docked, we all went out to lunch. When we finished, the prospect's wife kissed me on my forehead. She said I reminded her of her son. From that point on, we all had a totally different relationship. The sale was pretty much over as soon as we got off that boat. The competition still doesn't know why they didn't win that business.

Dealing with your prospects on a personal level does make a difference when you are selling or sailing. It also makes the job of selling more enjoyable. I enjoyed those folks from Sarasota. It's gratifying to establish friends as you are doing business. When it is all about business, there's no fun, no creativity, and everyone is more inflexible and stuffy. People have their guard up, and the entire experience becomes much more of a grind. All the people you come across will have something about them that you can find to like. This is essential, because you have to show and have a sincere concern for your people's best interest.

FEED YOUR CREATIVE MIND

There's little joy in being average, so let's not be like every other salesperson on the planet. This doesn't mean go out and get body pierced, or inked up from head to toe with some wild design. I am speaking to productive creativity. The first step is to be conscious, able thinking, and active in a creative way. So you might be thinking, "Great, that's easy, but now what?" We have already discussed several ways to be creative during large blocks of time or on the go. Let's run down this lane a little further. One of the things you can do is start a creative file. It takes remarkably little effort or time. Anytime you see an ad, a magazine title for an article, or anything that strikes you as creative, just stick in it a file. Soon your file will be full of other people's creativity. Yes, it's theirs, and you have to find your own. But other things you see that strike you or stand out in some way will feed your creative mind. It's kind of a mental kick-start. Here's just one example of what I am talking about.

NOT YOUR FATHER'S APPROACH

My editor and I were kicking around potential subtitles for this book, so I pulled out my creative file.

One ad that struck me as brilliant was an old Oldsmobile ad. From the marketing campaign, the company was obviously trying to attract younger buyers. Oldsmobile had retooled several of its cars to be more geared to the younger generation. The ads, you might recall, said, "This is not your father's Oldsmobile."

That ad stood out to me as being creative, and at the same time, it delivered a powerful message. In a nutshell, it was telling us this is a new type of Oldsmobile. Whatever you thought before is different, and we have changed, was the message. That was the same kind of message I wanted to communicate about the Transformational QPQ Selling approach detailed in this book. I wanted my subtitle to be, "This Is Not Your Father's Sales Approach." With all my creative wisdom, I thought that was an excellent approach. A lot of salespeople sell the same way their fathers did fifty years earlier, which is not optimal in today's economy. I thought it was a perfect message to convey.

Unfortunately, my editor didn't like it. I never said all my ideas were good. He thought there might be issues from Oldsmobile if we used it. He also said our approach was more along the Mercedes-Benz style, not Oldsmobile. He had a few other expert comments that rained on my parade. Hey, I still like it. The point is that when I went into my creative file, my mind was flooded with all kinds of ideas and thoughts. By just looking at other creative images and captions, your creative mind will turn on.

CREATIVITY NOT REALIZED

Another effective approach that requires about five seconds of effort is to start a creative journal. Write down your random thoughts in a notebook. It doesn't matter what they are. The key to having creativity work for you is, you have to act on your ideas every once in a while. Being creative, or to be creative without acting on innovative thoughts, is meaningless.

I had a great idea about twenty years ago. I have had a few others since then, but this one makes my point. I thought how lucrative it would be to *sell season tickets to watch your favorite football team's games on TV*. I thought people would pay to watch their favorite team on TV if they were out of their viewing area. My thinking was that when I moved to Atlanta from Cincinnati, I would have loved to watch the Bengals play on Sundays. Every NFL game is televised somewhere, so why not sell packages to all the other people who have moved and who still wanted to follow their favorite teams on cable TV? Sounds like a fantastic idea, doesn't it? It must have been a solid and creative idea, because today it's called DirecTV's *NFL Sunday Ticket*. Guess how much I earned off my creative idea? Nothing.

It's great to have a journal of creative ideas, but you have to pull it out once in a while and act on them. A current idea in my journal and one I want to act on is to have all the water in your shower drain into a reserve tank in the yard. All the used water can be recycled and run through the sprinkler system to water your lawn. Don't steal that one; come up with your own.

Creativity breeds new and fresh thoughts. It's the actions you take and the execution of your thoughts that breed success. All businesses were started with the entre-preneurial spirit of creativity. Regardless of the current size of the organization—IBM, AT&T, or Coke—they all started with a single creative idea someone acted on. Interview the most successful person you know and ask him/her if he/she regularly acted on his/her own creativity. Successful people know the value of employing creativity. You can transform your results by applying creativity to all aspects of your personal and professional life.

CHAPTER 8

TRANSFORMATION IN COMMUNICATION SOCIAL MEDIA

ADOPTERS

With the advent of social media, methods of communication continue to evolve and transform. By far, a salesperson's most significant challenge is finding qualified opportunities. Of course, it would be outstanding if the company she/he works for has such a successful market machine that leads are in abundance. Personally, I have not heard of that situation occurring often, especially lately. In the world we live in, people are put into one of four categories. You are an early adopter, middle adopter, late adopter, or nonadopter.

An early adopter is the person who wants to be the first one to try anything new. Early adopters tend to want to be the first person, or one of the first people, to have the latest and greatest thing. My friend Dave is an early adopter. He always has the latest version of the iPhone and Apple laptop, and recently he just bought a new electric car. A year before Tesla could deliver their new Model S, Dave sent them an $80,000 deposit. When he did this, he didn't know if Tesla would be able to deliver the Model S. He certainly didn't know at the time that the Model S would be voted Car of the Year by *Motor Trend* magazine. Dave read all about the car and bought it.

I want to believe I am middle adopter. Middle adopters tend to see if the product works and will catch on before they commit to buying or using something. These people are never first in line, but they are far from the last to try something new.

Dave took me to the Tesla dealership to show me the prototype Model S. I will admit I loved it! I could not find one thing I didn't like about the car, except it only goes three hundred miles per charge. The size, the style, the technology—it is an awesome car! Being a middle adopter, many thoughts and questions blocked my desire to have a Model S in the first production run. Will Tesla deliver the Model S? Once it becomes more accepted, will the price drop? It will be better for me when they have more charging stations in my area. How reliable will the car be? How easy will it be to get repairs? All these are reasonable thoughts and questions, but an early adopter doesn't care. He/she feels the benefits far outweigh any risk.

The later adopters are the people who resist change at all cost. These are the people who buy something new when it is not new anymore. Their way of doing anything is satisfactory, so they see no need to change. There might be better ways, easier ways, and more advanced ways, but they just won't change until it is required. If it's not broken, why fix it, or if it's working well enough, why change? My father was a classic example of a late adopter. My dad watched TV on a twenty-five-inch console television from 1970. When I would go to visit him, I would sit on the couch and look down to watch a program on this tiny screen with this big piece of furniture around it. You can buy a forty-two-inch flat-screen TV these days for about $400 or less. I would complain every time I was at my dad's house, "Dad, let's go get you a new TV." I even offered to buy it! Every time he would give me a gruff and offended tone and say, "What's wrong with this one?" I gave up when the picture finally died, and he actually paid $200 to have his relic of a TV repaired!

My father was a borderline nonadopter. He did use email, so he barely makes it into the late-adopter category. A nonadopter just won't change. Can you imagine not using email and going to the post office to send a letter every time you wanted to reach out to your prospects? How much have your personal and business lives transformed by having a cell phone? There are people in the world today who do not have a cell phone or use email. Let's agree these people are probably not successful salespeople.

Which category describes you best? To be fair, you might be an early adopter in some areas and a late or nonadopter in another. You might be the person first in line to buy any advancement in technology, which makes you an early adopter. On the another hand, you might only be cold calling and using direct mail off some random list of contacts to find prospects. You might be selling the same way you did years ago and have not transformed at all. That's not as bad as my dad's 1970s TV, but it does make you a late or a nonadopter. Being a late adopter in the sales profession will cost you a lot of money. You will work too hard and not be as productive, and your growth will be stymied.

My friend Ed is a successful attorney. Attorneys have to find new clients if their businesses are going to grow and thrive. Every time I turn on the TV, there is Ed with another commercial. When I drive down the street, I see Ed's picture on a billboard promoting his services. I can only imagine how much money he spends on these mediums to get the word out about his law firm. It is not practical for most salespeople to use TV or billboards. Cold calling and direct mail are still popular methods to find prospects. There are, however, more prudent and cost-effective approaches that can be applied through social media today for salespeople to transform their results. Today prospects will often use their computer, smartphone, or tablet using a web-based search engine to find where to go for solutions to their issues.

BLOGGING

A blog is an informal information site where you can publish your own material and send it out over the web. A typical blog combines text, images, and links to other blogs, web pages, and other media related to its topic. The best blogs offer the ability for readers to leave comments in an interactive format. It is helpful to give readers the ability to offer you feedback on the material you are sending out.

In the simplest terms, a blog is nothing more than your own personal newsletter or informational letter sent to people who subscribe to your blog. You will likely start with your own email list of clients and prospects, and they will have the option to continue receiving information from you or opt out of your blog. This is a substantial transformation in communication. You don't have to go to a printing company and pay it for design services or printing. The cost is very low, compared with paying for postage and printing. Sending out information on your blog is instant, where a mailed newsletter could take up to a week to be received. You can also get instant feedback on your blog posts. In sales terms, that can mean finding an interested new prospect.

Make sure your blog adds value to your clients' and prospects' lives. Otherwise, it will be perceived as junk mail, and you'll end up blocked as spam, and you'll have the opposite effect on your prospects than you planned.

It is important to blog frequently, but not too frequently to be an annoyance—once a week is plenty. Same issue, if you blog too often, you'll be marked as spam.

Do you have your own personal blog? I'll assume most of you answered no. My question is, "Why don't you?" At the end of the day, the only person you can count on for success is yourself. It is a mistake to hope your marketing organization generates enough leads for you to meet your financial goals. We have discussed the need to be a trusted advisor to your clients and prospects. One of the easiest ways to be thought of as an expert in anything is to publish useful information. When you are writing your content for your blog, make sure you have plenty of key words in the body of your communications. Key words are the terms you want to pop up if a potential prospect is searching for a solution to his/her issues.

Imagine what an advantage you would have in a selling situation if you had been sending out useful information on your blog to a client or prospect. Your competition shows up and does little more than regurgitate the company's marketing message. You will have a huge advantage that the competitor will not overcome, provided your solution can meet the prospect's need. Combine this with the Transformational QPQ Sales approach and you will win every time!

HOW TO CREATE A BLOG

The good news is that once you set up your blog, sending out posts is quick and easy. I will give you some basics of how to set up your own blog, but there are tons of sites on the internet if you Bing or Google this question with step-by-step instructions. Here are your basic steps:

1. **Differentiate.** There are a lot of blogs, so you have to decide specifically what your blog is going to be about and who you will target as your readers. Of course, you want to target your clients and prospects. Do you want to target Dilbert and all his cousins or do you want to target the "C" suite? Depending on what you are selling and the information you provide, targeting Dilbert is not a bad thing. Here's a crazy thought: have two different blogs.

2. **Choose WordPress.** Sign up for this free software that will allow you to host your own domain name.

3. **Create your domain name:** It will cost you about $30 a year to host your own domain. You have already decided on the target audience and your subject, so selecting a domain name should be easy.

4. **Select a web host:** Dream Host (Dreamhost.com) is a good site to get you started. It offers easy, one-click installation. It will cost you about $120 a year,

but your investment in your own success is worth it. Go Daddy (godaddy.com) is another good option for you to consider. Both sites provide domain-name search capabilities to ensure no one else has your domain.

5. **Install/configure WordPress:** This could take you anywhere from five minutes to forty-five minutes, depending on your experience level. There are step-by-step instructions within WordPress that any novice can follow. It is in this step where you select your user name, password, look and feel, themes, and so on for your blog.

That's it. Now you have no excuse for not having your own blog. It will take you an hour or less and cost you maybe $150 a year. Your return on investment will be well worth the time and cost! Think about how much just one new account is worth to you.

NETWORKING CONTACTS

Years ago, the only way to get prospect contact information was to buy a list of random names, addresses, and phone numbers. I cannot tell you how many hours I spent calling wrong numbers, asking for people who had left the company, and following up on wrong data. Today some lists now offer email addresses that are occasionally accurate. It would be a perfect world if you could actually select your target market, select the titles you wanted to target, and then get accurate emails, phone numbers, and names. Acquiring any outside list is costly, and the data is time sensitive and is often outdated. This has been an issue for salespeople and marketing organizations for years. Prudently managing your network contacts has transformed with tools like LinkedIn.

LINKEDIN

LinkedIn is a social networking site for professionals. Unlike Facebook, which is a social website mostly for casual and personal use, or business-to-consumer use, LinkedIn is focused on professional networking. Almost two hundred million professionals subscribe to LinkedIn. There are other professional social networking sites, like Viadeo and Xing, but LinkedIn is by far the largest. LinkedIn is used to maintain a list of contacts and details on people with whom you have some level of relationship. These are called connections. You can invite anyone to become a connection. You can also use LinkedIn to find people, get exact titles of people, and find contact information. You will find just about everyone using LinkedIn has a profile, which is a resume that offers a lot of useful background information.

This list of connections can then be used in many different ways.

Users can upload their resumes or design their own profiles to display work history and professional experiences. This clearly shows their professional experience and expertise. LinkedIn can then be used to find jobs, people, and business opportunities recommended by someone in one's contact network. I often tell salespeople that if they would spend more time networking when they had a job to find more qualified prospects, they wouldn't need to network to find a new job!

A contact network can contain your direct connections, the connections of each of your connections (referred to as second-level connections), and also the connections of second-level connections (referred to as third-level connections). This can be used to get introductions to someone you want to reach through a mutual contact. Everyone knows someone. It is often surprising who the people you know are in contact with. LinkedIn will help you leverage others' contacts who are willing to help you when asked.

As a subscriber to LinkedIn, you can post your photo and view photos of others to help you recognize people. You can now follow different companies and get notifications about the new people hired and offerings that become available. Sending out a note or email to your prospect when the latest news is announced is a good practice to get in the habit of doing regularly.

LEVERAGING YOUR PROFESSIONAL NETWORK

Do you already have a LinkedIn account? Unlike my question about whether you have a personal blog, I will assume you answered yes. If you didn't answer yes, put this book down and go sign up. The real question is, "Are you leveraging LinkedIn, Viadeo, or Xing to get more business?" I know a lot of salespeople who have an account on one of these sites, but do almost nothing with it. What is the point of having an account if you are not using the tool?

Assuming you have an account and a number of connections, the next thing I would suggest is to get your connections to write a short recommendation for you. This will give you credibility when someone is deciding to connect with you or do business with you in the future.

LinkedIn has a question-and-answer section you should leverage. This allows you to send out questions to experts and connect with them at the same time. You cannot have enough mavens in your network. Mavens know a lot of other mavens who can help you and can refer you to potential prospects.

Another way to expand your network is to utilize the group section of LinkedIn, called LinkedIn Groups. This section allows you to connect with likeminded people. For salespeople, this can be other salespeople. I have to remind salespeople all the time that there are other salespeople who call on the same accounts as they do but aren't competitors. These other salespeople might have contacts you want and need. They might have insight into the account that would be useful for you. You might have useful information that you can help a fellow salesperson with as well. The sales community in general needs to work closer together to help one another. Using LinkedIn Groups is a good way to start the ball rolling. You have to invest some time and measure your results for the time you spend on LinkedIn, Viadeo, or Xing. Just like anything in life, you get back what you put into it.

Higher financial commitment to LinkedIn gains you more access to people, information, and search capabilities. Monthly commitment can range from $25 to $75. LinkedIn subscription variables include the number of monthly LinkedIn emails (InMail) to prospects, search, and drill-down capabilities. You can gain search filters on company type and size, LinkedIn member company positions/titles, interests, and groups, and you can connect with second- and third-tier connections.

Connect to as many people as you can. Your network will expand exponentially as you add LinkedIn connections. You will have access to detailed information on LinkedIn members who are connections of your LinkedIn network. A great practice is to send an InMail to a LinkedIn member prospect who is also connected to one of your connections (second tier). Introduce yourself as a friend or business associate of your mutual connection.

Another great networking method on LinkedIn is the use of groups. As of this writing, there are nearly 1.5 million groups on LinkedIn, some open to anyone, and some that are members only and require a group administrator's acceptance of your request to join to allow you into the group. Once in a group, you can search for members of the group and post messages to members of the group, which is essentially the same thing as a blog post. Spend some time researching the groups to determine which are best for you, meaning which networks your prospects are following. Join those groups and stay active in them. Make sure to get daily or weekly updates about others' posts and place your own posts once every week or so. Become the expert whom people like to follow by making valuable posts for the group.

ONLINE VIDEOS

Some people don't like to read. YouTube allows anyone to post a video about anything anytime he/she wants. To augment your blog, add video clips addressing the issues you have already written about. This is just another way to get a following and add to your trusted-advisor status. Keep in mind, someone, and hopefully a lot of people, will be viewing your posts. Make sure you are as professional and articulate as if you were addressing an audience of one hundred people in person.

UPLOADING YOUR ONLINE VIDEOS

The first thing you need to post a video on the web is a digital video camera. In years gone by, these video cameras could cost upward of $5,000. With the transformation in communications, even iPhones now have digital video recording capabilities. I will assume you have some sort of recording device available to use.

The next thing you need is a fire wire that plugs into your camera and the back of your computer. As soon as you plug the cord in, an icon will pop up on your computer that says, "Record." A box should also pop up where you add your headings and the subject you are recording. Once you have made your recording, you put it into a digital folder just like any other document you might save.

At this point, you are ready to post your video to YouTube. You can detach your fire wire and camera now. Simply go to YouTube and you will see a heading that says, "Upload." Click on it and a subject and description box will pop up. Put in your description, making sure you have the key words you think your prospects will search for when looking for information. You will also want to do this again in the section called, "Tags," which are the key words that will pop when someone is searching a particular subject. All that is left is to browse your folder and upload it to YouTube. The only other button you want to select is who you want to view the video. I suggest you select, "Public" so anyone can watch it.

Depending on how long it takes to record your video—I would suggest five minutes or less—this entire process will take you about ten minutes. Your recordings will stay on the web for years, and you might be surprised when one day out of the blue you find a new prospect who watched what you had to say and contacts you for more information. If you don't put yourself out there, then rest assured it will be much harder for people to find you.

GOOGLE ALERTS

Using Google Alerts is another way to keep track of people and organizations you are selling to. I will assume you know how to search on Google, so no need to spend time on that. Google Alerts will send you an email each time something is posted about the company or person you are following. To set this up, all you have to do is go to http://www.google.com/alerts. This will bring you to the Google Alerts home page. Type in the person or company you want to follow, and you're done! Now you can be instantly notified when breaking news is posted. You can react swiftly and sensibly each time to learn something new.

Be an adopter of the transformation in communication. You should be blogging, leveraging LinkedIn daily, posting informative videos on YouTube, and following your prospects on Google. Some people will also use Facebook and Twitter to get the word out about themselves and solutions. In my experience, those mediums are not as effective for business-to-business solutions. I have used both with limited success. Regardless, in today's transformed world of communications, prospects want to do business with trusted advisors they view as experts. There are so many options available today that people spend more time selecting who they feel is the right person or organization for the job. You have to differentiate yourself and make it easy for people to find you. Once they find you, you have to be a credible alternative for them to consider. It is a mistake to depend on your organization to do this for you. There is a lot of information on the web and in your local bookstore about social media. This chapter only offers you the tip of the iceberg of the things you can do to promote yourself and the solutions you provide. If you haven't already, it's time to aggressively transform how you communicate with clients and to find new prospects.

CHAPTER 9

HANDLING OBJECTIONS

In Chapter 3, we briefly discuss phase four of the QPQ sales approach. There is a lot more to be said about handling objections. Many sellers feel objections are obstacles or impediments in their sales cycle. Objections are nothing more than an opportunity to clarify a concern, issue, doubt, or some area of hesitation. A sales objection is a reluctance, indecision, or struggle to move forward. Objections can present great opportunities to sell. Objections are part of every sales cycle, yet I have not come across any sales team that has been formally trained in how to manage them. I have done many talks on this subject, and we even provide a one day workshop on this topic. "Obstacles don't have to stop you. If you run into a wall, don't turn around or give up. Figure out how to climb it, go through it or around it."

Michael Jordan

Making Cookies

How you handle objections is like making cookies. There are several ingredients required to make cookies. You need flour, eggs, brown sugar, and butter to name a few. If you use too much or not enough, of any of these, your cookies will not taste good. You have to have just the right mix. Another variable that is important is the baking time. If you bake your cookies too long they get burned. Not enough time, and they are too chewy. Just like baking cookies there is a process and required ingredients to be successful in handling objections. If you skip over or leave out one of the ingredients you might spoil your opportunity. If you react too defensively to an objection it is equivalent to over baking. Let's look at the proper recipe for handling objections.

Objection Phases

Whether you are making cookies, playing golf, or following a prudent sales approach, there are certain phases you need to follow to be successful. For example in golf, you wouldn't tee off on a long par 5 with a pitching wedge and have any chance of making par.

The same is true for handling objections. The proper phases are:

> ### Objection Phases
> - Categorize the Objection
> - Reason for the Objection
> - Accept the Objection
> - Define the Right Approach

Phase 1: Categorize the Objection

There are two types of objections. They fall into the category of authentic or fake. The authentic objection is easy. This is a real concern that has some validity to it. A real or authentic objection needs to be overcome and dealt with directly. You have a clearer picture of what the prospect is concerned about and is really looking for. Now you can present a more suitable solution that meets their needs and addresses their concerns. These genuine objections might be in the area of costs, misconceived notions about something, the reliability of your solutions and a host of other areas. For example, if a prospect heard that your product breaks down frequently and your organization's service is unreliable, that is a real concern. It doesn't matter if that perception is true or not. You have to addresses this directly. The more factual data you can provide the easier it will be to address and overcome real objections. Back to our example; if you were able to provide a press release about an award the company just won for product reliability and the excellent service the company provides to the prospect the objections they had would be easy to overcome.

Fake Objections are often nothing more than the prospect or client testing you. They might not have an authentic objection. They are challenging you to see how you react. Typical areas for fake objections are:

- Pricing/Discount
- Return on Investment (ROI) Claims
- Value Propositions
- Functionality/Technology Statements
- Support Response Times
- Delivery Dates

Fake objections can also be an avoidance tactic by your client or prospect. If you have been engaged in a long sales cycle with a prospect or have had a long affiliation with a client, you will form a relationship. Using avoidance tactics with fake objections is when you get excuses, create obstacles, delays the pursuit, and the opportunity is stalled. The typical reasons include:

• Avoiding Conflict
• Hiding something
• Like you and don't want to hurt your feelings
• Internal Politics

You have to be able to recognize the reasons you are getting a fake objection and make it easy for your prospect or client to share what the real issue is. You do this by assessing the situation and the objection, then exploring with your prospect/client one of these areas you feel the objection is coming from. If you shine a light on the area where the objection is coming from, then it is easier for them to talk about it with you openly and honestly.

Phase 2: Reasons for the Objections

There can be unlimited reasons for an objection. They can range from the client wants what they want to a serious concern about something. Let's try to narrow that down a bit. I believe there are 6 basic reasons for objections.

The 6 Basic Reasons for Objections

The Prospect/client:
- Doesn't feel understood
- Doesn't understand
- Is using you
- Doesn't believe you
- Is attempting to hide something
- Is not a qualified opportunity

Prospect/Client doesn't feel understood is very typical today. People buy because they feel understood not because they understand. That fact has been repeated so many times by so many people it is hard to determine who said it first. This statement has never been truer than it is today. What I find most sales people doing though is spending large amounts of time trying to get the prospect to understand. We want to tell them about the features and benefits of our solution and feel if they understand that thoroughly enough, then they will buy. It is not all the sales person's fault we go down this path. When a new sales person joins a company the orientation is almost always about the solutions they will be selling and almost never about understanding the people they will be selling to. You'll get a lot less objections if you understand the person you are selling to.

Prospect/Client doesn't understand what you are offering them; of course objections are soon to follow. If a prospect doesn't understand something, this is principally due to explanations or lack of acceptable information. To avoid this, constantly check to see that the prospect understands what you are talking about. I will often stop in the middle of a presentation or an explanation of something and ask the simple questions; Are you with me? Am I being clear? Does that make sense? This will really help ensure that everyone is on the same page and there is not confusion.

When the prospect/client is using you, they often create a lot of fake objections. If you haven't been used by someone in a sales situation, just wait, you will. I have cited a few examples of this in the previous chapters. The project leader at 3M was using me to fill in his matrix of vendors and the requirement he had to have two presenters in Singapore. Prospects will use you to leverage a price with their current vendor, to get educated on the latest developments, and justify that they considered other alternatives to their current situation. Once you recognize you are being used, it will be clear to you how to address objections you might get. This is especially true when applying the QPQ sale approach. If the prospect is giving you little or nothing in return for what you are offering, they are likely using you and have no intention of buying from you.

If prospect/client doesn't believe you, is another reason you will get objections. You need to be a trusted advisor, relate to the prospect at their level, (QPQ), then back up claims with specific evidence. This will confirm what has been said, written, or presented. The more empirical data you can provide the more believable you will be.

When the prospect/client is attempting to hide something, they will stir up all kind of objections. There are several things they could be hiding from you. The typical list includes, they:
- Aren't really the decision maker.
- Have a bias and you are just a vendor in the matrix.
- Lost their funding.
- Lost an internal political battle.
- Don't like you.

You can rarely overcome an objection from a prospect that isn't qualified. A prospect would be considered not qualified if they have lost funding, you are not talking to right person, or they have a strong bias for someone else. We have to ask the hard questions up front and be prepared to deal with the reality.

Phase 3: Accepting the Objection

In relationship management courses or conflict management courses one of the first things they advise you to do is to accept what you are hearing. You need to listen, and fully take in what the prospect/client is saying to you. By listening without immediately reacting, you are accepting the objection. This lets them share more about their concerns without feeling pressured by a knee jerk reaction. This creates mutual trust and collaboration. Don't fall into the trap, thinking: "I've got to counter this objection to make a sale" by immediately reacting in a defensive way. Just like with anything there are do's and don'ts.

Objection Don'ts

- Immediately respond
- Interrupt
- Tune them out
- Assume

- Over react
- Get an attitude
- Create conflict

Phase 4: Define the Right Approach

There are several schools of thought on the right approach to handle objections. I firmly believe the list below is what you need to do to address objections effectively.

HANDLING OBJECTIONS

1. Develop the Right Attitude
2. Anticipate
3. Playback
4. Explore the Reasoning
5. Confirm

The first thing to in keep in mind is your attitude about the objection. What you should consider is taking the approach that every real objection is a concern of some sort. Step outside of the business world for a minute and think how you react when someone offers you a legitimate concern about something. Most of us listen closely, try to be understanding, and address it in a non-confrontational way. We tend to react much differently to an objection vs. a real concern. Often times we see an objection as a personal challenge of some sort, which is the wrong approach. That can lead to confrontation, miscommunication, and an emotional response.

Another approach to address objections I am a big proponent of, is to anticipate prospect's objections and address them in advance. Putting yourself in the prospect's shoes and addressing potential concerns before they bring them up will give you credibility.

Play back the objection as you understand it. Repeat back to your prospect the essence of what you think you heard and the potential reason why they have the objection. "I understand it's not the cost, it's the resources and time to implement..." This shows that you were listening and gives the prospect a chance to clarify.

Explore the potential reasons for the objection. Before answering an objection, ask a few exploratory questions that will allow the prospect to share more about their concerns and feelings. You only want to address an objection once, so let them get out all their issues before you address them.

When it is time to actually address the objection, your goal is to relieve their concerns, misconceived notions, and move forward. After you have appropriately addressed the objection, confirm that you've answered the objection and everyone is on the same page.

Skipping any of these steps or trying to take a short cut when handling objections can be disaster. Follow these guidelines and you will soon welcome objections. You will realize you are much closer to making a sale.

CHAPTER 10

TROUBLESOME TRUTH

During a period of transformation, the truth is troublesome and is often ugly. This is true whether the transformation is organizational or personal. Regardless of the tactics, strategies, and processes offered through a transitional phase, transformation is difficult. It is challenging for any of us to admit we need to change. The more we have invested in something, the more we want for it to work. As a salesperson, this investment is often time, energy, people, approaches, and processes.

THE PROCESS

Life has its own flows, rhythms, and timeframes. Nothing happens when we want it to. This is especially true for sales professionals. Sellers are under constant pressure for results. Even if a salesperson has closed a new client, the question soon comes, "What have you done lately?" Because of this, salespeople sometimes force the buying process.

It would be easy to be confused by the statement "sales professionals should not force the buying process" and what you have read about Transformational QPQ Selling. These two statements might seem to be in conflict with each other. They are very different.

QPQ is designed to help sellers control the sales cycle, not force the process. There are many hungry salespeople who are borderline desperate to make a sale.

The common scenario usually starts when the seller's pipeline of prospects is weak. The seller finds a prospect who meets the first criteria for the basics of qualification, "has a need the seller can meet." The salesperson then forces the process, being too aggressive in calling the prospect, pushing for presentations prematurely, and trying to close the business. This is stereotypical quota salesperson behavior. This is the opposite of the trusted-advisor approach that is required for today's markets.

Transformational QPQ Selling encourages salespeople to be professionally assertive. Of course, the approach helps shorten the sales cycle. The process establishes a give-and-take relationship where salespeople negotiate to take out unnecessary steps in the sales cycle. QPQ also gives sellers a professional way to get to the top person as a trusted advisor. Pushy, desperate salespeople will not be consistently successful. Sellers need to sort out early in a pursuit if they have a qualified opportunity, which requires understanding buyers' timeframes. *There are three elements to the buying process. They are timeframes, solution fit, and acceptance of the logic the solution offers.*

TIMEFRAMES

Prospects' timeframes need to be understood and validated. Understanding the compelling reason they are considering something different will help you sort out their real timeframe to buy. Attempting to accelerate timeframes is often a mistake because salespeople can come across as desperate or self-serving in their approach. I have heard salespeople tell prospects things like they need to close their sale by a certain date so the seller can qualify for the club trip. Another thing that doesn't come across well is saying it's the end of the quarter or end of the year, and the company needs to book the business. There are many more statements just like these that hurt a seller's ability to generate results.

A more professional approach would be to execute phase three in the QPQ process, which frames things in a way that's good for the prospect. At the end of the day, everything has to be said in a way that implies the prospect is the one who receives all the benefit. It's OK to say something like, "Signing the agreement before the fifteenth will ensure that you get the resources you want scheduled. This will make it easier for you to meet your go-live dates." That is much better than "we need to make our numbers."

FIT

Forcing the process sometimes means trying to sell someone a solution that will not completely meet his/her needs. You will probably be successful doing that once. In sales terms, that is referred to as forcing a square peg into a round hole. It's just not going to work. You might plug the hole, but not very well.

We are fortunate enough to have a solid referral network of transformed clients. One of my best clients called me to let me know he had referred our services to a colleague who needed help in the area of negotiating. That is something we can help clients with. When I called and talked to this person, I discovered what he needed was something much different than what we offered. He had a very small company. His team needed the most basic negotiating-skills training. I could have put something together, overcharged him, and generated some revenue for our company. It was more prudent for me to refer him to some online courses I felt would meet his needs. He was so appreciative of this approach that he referred me to a prospect who needed someone to come in and assess why his company wasn't growing. This turned out to be a much better and bigger opportunity for us. Sellers should not force the process for short-term gain. They should take a longer view and sincerely help prospects solve their business issues.

UNDISPUTED LOGIC

The last part of the process is the logic aspect of selling. What I propose sales professionals focus on selling is undisputed logic.

Undisputed logic is the compelling and logical reasons to buy your solution.

Undisputed logic is facts and reasons that a person would be foolish to debate. If you have presented such well-thought-out logic and proof that you can help a prospect, and he/she still does not move to action, perhaps it is time to find another sales opportunity. We have had two recent clients who offered prospects guaranteed, hard-dollar ROIs (returns on investment). If their solution doesn't save the prospect X amount of money, then the company writes the prospect a check at the end of the year! If you can't sell free, you can't sell!

Once a prospect is presented with the compelling business case and then guaranteed results, he/she should buy. If the prospect hesitates, delays, or doesn't make a decision, then something is broken with the sales process or approach. Most sellers can't offer guarantees like this, but they can offer logical solutions to business problems.

Sometimes salespeople have trouble framing solutions in a logical way, so it is not easy for buyers to realize the undisputed logic. Salespeople who approach prospects by regurgitating the marketing literature usually aren't selling undisputed logic. On the other side, if a prospect has identified an issue, and he/she has been offered a logical and prudent solution and doesn't act, then you have to look at the inconvenient truth of the situation, which is that this is not a prospect.

Over the years, we have encountered many prospects who tell us they need to raise their revenues. After a thorough investigation, it is determined the client needs a new sales approach, new processes, and sometimes people with different skills. The maddening part of this is when the prospect completely agrees with the assessment and then says, "We need to increase the revenues before we can follow any of your recommendations." That makes no sense. A classic question applies here: Which comes first, the chicken or the egg? The revenues won't increase until the organization adopts some of the recommendations and makes some changes. But the company won't move forward until its revenues increase. There's no logic to this type of thinking. If you have presented undisputed logic and your logic is ignored, one of three things has occurred:

1. The logic has been presented to someone who doesn't care or can't make a decision.
2. For whatever reason, the prospect doesn't believe you.
3. The prospect isn't interested in solving the issue.

Regardless, whatever the reason is, it's futile to continue to force the process when someone isn't ready to buy.

TRANSFORMATION IN COURAGE

Everything up to this point in this book requires some level of courage. Most sellers will need a transformation in their courage level to execute the tactics and concepts that you have read about. Everything we do today requires courage.

It takes courage, among other things, to write a book. In my opinion, there are many more people who have the ability to write a book. They never follow through for some of the same excuses that hold them back from achieving many other things in their lives. The real reason might be lack of courage. The thoughts start creeping in while I'm writing: What if people don't like this book? What if people don't agree with my thoughts? What if no one buys my book? What if I look like a fool? The questions are endless and can be intimidating. Personally, I would rather face the music of all these very real possibilities rather than not try to convey my thoughts, or offer a fresh perspective to selling. For me, the potential rewards far outweigh the risk.

The same complacent attitudes that hold an individual seller back can affect a company's success and growth as well. How many times have you heard, "If it's not broken, why fix it?" Aging product lines, lack of an investment in people, outdated solutions, and lack of vision to the changing needs in the marketplace are death sentences to a company's ability to grow.

Someone at McDonald's showed some real courage and took a risk when he/she proposed offering a breakfast menu. McDonald's was doing well before it offered a breakfast menu. What if no one came to McDonald's for breakfast? McDonald's is not known for breakfast. There are many other restaurants that offer breakfast. I can almost hear the corporate executives, who are typically risk averse, expressing all the reasons why the breakfast idea wouldn't work. No one can say for certain who originated the quote, "No guts, no glory" that exemplifies courageous action. You have to be willing to try new things if you want any type of transformation in your results.

QPQ COURAGE

You have read about applying QPQ, the strategic withdrawal, moving out of Dilbertville, and a host of other new ideas. Some of you might think these ideas are too risky to adopt. There are others reading this right now who can't wait to apply the approach to sales pursuits they are working. The difference between the two is often the level of courage each possesses.

I think most of you have heard that a lot of self-made millionaires make their fortune, lose it at some point, and then make it all back. At just a passing glance, that makes no sense, does it? How could a person work so hard and dedicate themselves to make a million dollars, or more, and then lose it? When you dig a little deeper it makes perfect sense. Self-made millionaires have to take some risks and show lots of courage. Through their courage, vision, and hard work, they "made it." They continue to improve themselves and extend their reach. They don't allow themselves to become complacent. They continuously apply a risk and reward formula to success. Just because you have courage doesn't mean you will achieve your ultimate goal. Courage alone, without applying the other aspects of success, doesn't ensure success. There are no guarantees in anything. When these self-made millionaires reach out for a goal, they can come up empty. Even worse, they may find themselves in serious financial difficulties. The interesting thing is that self-made millionaires can make their millions, lose their millions, and then make it all back again. You might think you would be too depressed and too discouraged, or would find reasons to quit. If that were the makeup of these millionaires, they wouldn't have achieved success in the first place. If they take a risk that somehow doesn't pay off, they apply the same principles of success and courage to take calculated risks to earn their millions back again.

Applying the QPQ approach to your sales engagements might not net you results the first few times you use the strategies. If you stick with them and dedicate yourself to mastering them they will transform your results.

WORDS OF WISDOM

Making mistakes is just part of the transformation process. When I was in my first sales position, I made a lot of mistakes. Everything I did just seemed to backfire. I was certain I was going to lose my job.

There was no doubt I was trying my hardest to succeed, though. One afternoon, I heard a big, booming voice shout out, "Beck, get in my office."

"Oh no," I thought. "This is it. I'm getting canned!" My boss at the time, Mr. Winton, told me to shut the door behind me, which only confirmed my suspicion. He could tell I was very nervous, and he asked what my problem was. I apologized for all my mistakes and reiterated how much I wanted to succeed. To my surprise, he laughed.

Mr. Winton then gave me some words of wisdom that will always stick with me. He said, "Let me tell you something, boy." (He liked to call me, "boy.") "I have been watching what you are doing, and you are making some mistakes. You are doing about three times as much as anyone else, though. The fact that you are making so many mistakes just shows me you're trying harder than anyone else. Most of those guys out there are just doing the same old thing and are going through the paces. I'm not worried in the least about you. I know you will sort out those mistakes, learn from them, and be the best salesperson we have very soon." He then handed me the keys to his brand-new Mercedes-Benz and told me to take it for a drive. When I graciously declined, he said, "I insist. I expect you to own one of these soon, so you should know how they drive."

Not everything was perfect in the organization. I could have easily gone into that office that day and started blaming everyone else for the issues I was having. If I had done that, you can bet the conversation would have gone in a different direction. I would not have gotten the words of wisdom he gave me. We all have to be honest about our failures. We have to learn from them and leverage the experiences to transform.

In my career, I have been in an executive role as president or vice president, with several people working under me. Each environment required consistent, predictable results. That mandate was handed down throughout the employee staff. Unfortunately, not everyone could achieve the level of results that were required, and those employees had to be let go. Without exception, their justification for their circumstances was that it was not their fault, and they should not be terminated. They would blame their lack of results on everything other than themselves. These people were not working hard, not committed to improving, were generally closed minded, not motivated to succeed, or offered very little creativity to their role.

THE BLAME GAME

Ask a salesperson how he/she secured that new account or won a large sale, and 99.9 percent of the time you will hear that superior salesmanship was what won the deal. He/she will likely go on and share his/her masterful strategy. He/she will share how he/she built relationships based on mutual respect with the decision maker. He/she will go on to talk about the creativity he/she applied while setting traps for the competitor throughout the sales cycle. Most salespeople will stop just short of pounding their chests.

Now ask the same person why he/she lost an opportunity, or why he/she is not achieving the required results. I will fall on the floor the first time I hear, "I wasn't good enough, I got sloppy, I skipped steps, or I got outsold." Instead, salespeople typically say it was the manager's fault, it was the tight market, the overpriced product, the lack of leads, or a host of other excuses. The fact is that if they had had the courage and looked at what areas they could improve in, their results would be different. If sellers pushed themselves to continue to learn new methods of selling, learn more about the market, or make sure they were not complacent, they could probably beat their chests in victory more often.

MOTIVATION

You were motivated enough to pick up this book and read. Because of that, I will assume you are open minded enough to try new things. These qualities, joined with applying the Transformation QPQ Sales approach, are enough to transform your results.

Jim Rohn, in *Motivational Quotes*, is credited with saying, "Motivation is a mystery. Why does one salesperson see his/her first prospect at 7:00 in the morning, while another salesperson is just getting out of bed at 9:00 a.m.? I don't know. It's part of the mysteries of life.

"Give a lecture to a thousand people. One walks out and says, 'I'm going to change my life.' Another one walks out with a yawn and says, 'I've heard all this before.' Why is that? Why wouldn't both be affected the same way? Another mystery.

"The millionaire says to a thousand people, 'I read this book, and it started me on the road to wealth.' Guess how many go out and get the book? Very few. Isn't that incredible? Why wouldn't everyone get the book? A mystery of life."

When I talk to groups of salespeople, one of the first things I do is predict the future. I predict that some will listen intently, some will take notes, some will ask questions, and some will say, "Been there, done that." The winners will take the material I have given them and read it over and over again until they absorb it thoroughly. They will integrate the concepts and tactics into everything they do in pursuit of better results. As a consequence, they become successful far beyond their expectations.

The same can be true for all of you who are reading this book right now. You're not reading just another how-to on selling. You're holding a million dollars. That's right, at least a million dollars. The good news is that if you faithfully follow the principles in this book, you'll earn at least a million dollars in your sales career. In fact, I want to challenge you to set the goal of earning a million dollars in just one year.

CRAZY THINKING

Is it crazy to think you could earn a million in one year? Does that sound crazy to you? When I was a senior at the University of Cincinnati, I took a résumé-writing class. One of the projects was to write your résumé and hand one out to everyone in the class. The class read the résumés and then decided which person they'd like to interview. Guess who they picked? I believe the reason I was picked was I made the mistake of typing my résumé on an electric typewriter with a script ball. (I'm sad to say this was before everyone had a laptop computer.)

So I sat up in front of the room, and the class lobbed questions at me. They were your basic interview questions, the ones that every rookie manager asks. One question was, "What are your short-term goals?" I promptly responded, "I'd like to earn $100,000 in one year, within three years of graduation." The class busted out laughing. I'm a pretty perceptive guy, but I had no clue what they were howling about. Finally, the teacher jumped in and said, "Bob, you really have to be more realistic with your goals. Do you realize the average wage for a college graduate is about $14,000 per year?" (This was in the 1980s.)

I was shocked that everyone thought my goal was so unrealistic. However, it turned out that in my third year out of school, my W-2 showed that I'd earned in excess of $100,000. Frankly, between you and me, I should have reached that level in my second year. I missed an opportunity or two…and I hadn't figured out the entire QPQ approach yet.

The point I want to make is that earning a million dollars in one year is not crazy thinking. It's an attainable goal, and you can do it if that's what you're committed to.

You have to set goals, envision yourself reaching them, and let nothing get in your way, especially your own thoughts of defeat. Be positive. Never give up. And you'll accomplish whatever your goals may be. Mark Twain said, "Twenty years from now, you will be more disappointed by the things you didn't do than by the things you did do."

TRANSFORMATION

My sincere hope for all of you is that the trade winds are always at your backs, and that you reach every destination you set your sights on!

About the Author

Bob Beck has over twenty-eight years of experience in creating, expanding, and running organizations, with an unsurpassed record of accomplishment. Having been on the ground floor with three self-funded startups as a senior executive, and having led their growth through IPOs, Bob is truly a unique resource. Bob is a former board member of a publicly traded software firm and has been an executive partner in several firms. As an executive partner, Bob leverages his expertise in helping with all aspects of growing the business. He was founder and former CEO of Sales Builders Inc. for twelve years before merging the company to create the Transition-Group, which is a dedicated professional-development firm with the mission of partnering with organizations to ensure they realize their full potential. By offering a wide variety of expertise, TG is focused on helping organizations transition, thrive, and improve their results. He developed the ever-popular and growing Transformational QPQ Selling series of training courses that has now been taught in ten countries. This results-oriented approach to selling is being used with unmatched results by many firms today. Beck has also started and sold two companies himself.

Beck is married, has four children, and holds a bachelor's of science degree from the University of Cincinnati.

In 2013, Beck authored his third book, *Transformation—Reinventing Selling for Breakthrough Results*, which offers a fresh perspective and results-oriented tactics all sales professionals can use to improve their results. In 2009 Beck authored the number-one best-selling book, *Winning in the Fifth Quarter*. This is an inspiring book about success, transformation, and the attributes of success that can be applied to all of our lives. Beck has worked with the National Football League (NFL) and its former players, helping them with the issues of transitioning from the game to transform their lives. In 2005 Beck authored his first book, *Mutual Respect*, which was aimed at helping salespeople break out of developing subservient relationships with prospects and clients. In 1999 Beck was asked to contribute to INC. magazine's book, *310 Great Ideas for Smarter Selling*. You can find Beck's philosophies and tactics profiled in many leading trade magazines, blogs, and radio programs. Whether you are the CEO of a Fortune 500 organization or a salesperson on the frontlines, Beck's books, CDs, and articles can be your guiding light to success!